NOT AT YOUR CHILD'S EXPENSE

NOT AT YOUR
CHILD'S
EXPENSE

—— A GUIDE ——
TO CONSTRUCTIVE PARENTING

JUDITH FITZSIMMONS

New York

NOT AT YOUR CHILD'S EXPENSE
A GUIDE TO CONSTRUCTIVE PARENTING

© 2015 **JUDITH FITZSIMMONS**.

Published in New York, New York, by Morgan James Publishing. Morgan James and The Entrepreneurial Publisher are trademarks of Morgan James, LLC. www.MorganJamesPublishing.com

The Morgan James Speakers Group can bring authors to your live event. For more information or to book an event visit The Morgan James Speakers Group at www.TheMorganJamesSpeakersGroup.com.

A **free** eBook edition is available with the purchase of this print book.

CLEARLY PRINT YOUR NAME ABOVE IN UPPER CASE

Instructions to claim your free eBook edition:
1. Download the BitLit app for Android or iOS
2. Write your name in **UPPER CASE** on the line
3. Use the BitLit app to submit a photo
4. Download your eBook to any device

ISBN 978-1-63047-505-5 paperback
ISBN 978-1-63047-506-2 eBook
Library of Congress Control Number:
2014920850

Cover Design by:
Rachel Lopez
www.r2cdesign.com

Interior Design by:
Bonnie Bushman
bonnie@caboodlegraphics.com

In an effort to support local communities and raise awareness and funds, Morgan James Publishing donates a percentage of all book sales for the life of each book to Habitat for Humanity Peninsula and Greater Williamsburg

Get involved today, visit
www.MorganJamesBuilds.com

Habitat
for Humanity®
Peninsula and
Greater Williamsburg
Building Partner

With every breath that I take and with every beat of my heart, this book is dedicated to the light in my soul, my precious daughter, Chelsea; always remember your Mamma loves you.

And in loving memory of my own mother, Marie Mazzeo Fitzsimmons

TABLE OF CONTENTS

INTRODUCTION

Things don't always go the way you think they will, and this story starts there. In 1991, my husband and I had been struggling with our marriage for quite a while and decided we should get a divorce. After all, we were childless, young, healthy, and ready to get out of this relationship which was making both of us unhappy. We actually discussed the details of the divorce in a rather civil way primarily because we were both so relieved we were finally going to get out of our shared misery. After this engaging divorce conversation that left us both comforted, we decided to celebrate our decision and engage in another activity. I know, I know, what was I thinking? Well, there was wine involved and evidently I wasn't thinking clearly.

Two months after our initial divorce discussion, I was on the way to the lawyer's office to finalize the paperwork when I became violently ill. I know you need no drum role to figure out what happened next. Don't rub it in, you're right. Here I was 38 years old, beyond the verge of a divorce, and pregnant for the first time in my life. I thought it was some type of cruel cosmic joke. Her father and I decided to give it another attempt, but 18 months after our daughter was born, we knew we should have kept with our plan to divorce.

This book is based on our experiences over the past 20 years. We are not psychologists and we are not experts in parenting. We are not saintly people from whom compassion flows easily. We are what you might call mainstream America people; middle-aged, hard-working, law-abiding people. We are just like you in many ways, but one thing that makes us different is we started the co-parenting role after the marriage was over in our minds. Therefore, we didn't struggle with confusing our marital issues with our parenting issues. We didn't have deep-seated anger, resentment, or hatred, which often occurs during a divorce. We really only had one thing in common; our commitment to our daughter.

Much of what you read in this book, you're going to roll your eyes at; I don't blame you, I rolled my eyes as they were happening. Much of what you read you may not believe; however, it is true. At least it is the truth from my perspective, the mother of this precious child. Fortunately, the father of this child has also read the book and believes that it conveys an accurate account of our joint commitment. I think the primary reason we were able to parent the way we did is because we did not have marital baggage to deal with. Therefore, as you read this book, please take care of yourself and invest the time to help you get to a place where you can make the commitment to your child(ren) to be the best parent you can be. Professional counseling is beneficial and can help you develop an open heart and mind.

Divorce is painful, divorce is ugly, divorce is hurtful, divorce is scary, divorce is emotionally destructive, divorce shatters your equilibrium, divorce forces financial adjustments, divorce can be devastating. Okay, are we clear on this? But divorce doesn't have to be a process damaging to everyone involved. With focus, clarity, and commitment, you can participate in a life-changing experience and come out the other side with love for yourself and your child, the ability to heal, and confidence to enjoy a rewarding and fulfilling life.

When and How to Use this Book

You want to refer to this book often and before a problem escalates. Be proactive, calm, open minded, and dedicated to finding a solution to meet the needs of everyone involved. When you encounter an instance for which you need guidance, check the table of contents to see if one or more topic(s) addresses your situation. Read each topic once, twice, maybe even three times to capture the entire essence of what is being said. If you don't find a specific topic that addresses your trepidation, close your eyes, pray for guidance, and drop your finger into the table of contents; wherever it lands, that is the topic you want to read.

Note to male readers, the writing would become very awkward if I tried to cover both genders simultaneously, so please bear with my female perspective. You will still get a great deal of information and insights, so keep reading.

Imagine this Scene

You have been divorced for two years. You and your former husband live hundreds of miles apart, so you mutually decide he is going to come to your home for a weekend every month to spend time with his daughter. You assist in paying the airfare, you greet him at the airport, ask about his life and he about yours, and you arrive at home in time to get your daughter off the school bus. She runs into her father's arms with a screeching yell of joy and then jumps into your arms with a smile and a hug. Later, you, your current husband-equivalent, your former husband, and your daughter sit down for dinner. You all hold hands, say a prayer, and enjoy the meal, talking about a variety of subjects, including his new wife and her son. At bedtime, each adult surrounds your child's bed, prayers again, hugs and kisses, and after she is asleep, your current partner and former husband decide to go out to shoot a game of pool.

Do you think I've just left the realm of reality and am telling you, instead, about a dream my daughter has had? Well, you're wrong. This is what happened in our home. Not every month, because some months my current husband-equivalent and I took advantage of the free babysitter to get away. However, when we were in town, then the scene I just described happened repeatedly. Were we out of our minds? Some say yes. Wasn't it a difficult and awkward situation? Absolutely, but we worked together to make it as comfortable as possible for everyone involved. You might be saying, "Not in my lifetime," but guess what, if you want to enjoy a truly rewarding life full of love, compassion, and joy, you just might find this scene taking place in your home.

Why Is This So Difficult for Us?

Having this type of exchange may be difficult because you have a history with your former spouse. He has probably done such vile things that you shouldn't treat him in a kind manner. I accept you have a history, and I also accept he has done things you don't like. But if you are intending to have a child-friendly relationship, for the sake of your children, then you had better start putting your thoughts about your former husband in the same category as you would a stranger at the store. They say we hurt most the ones we love the most or who mean the most to us. So if you are trying to distance yourself emotionally from your former spouse, don't give him any more anger or pain than you would a stranger.

You might want to try this. Every time you speak to or see your former husband, say a silent mantra, "You are someone I used to love, you are someone I no longer need to love, you are someone I have to deal with, but you can't have any more of me than I am willing to give, and right now I will give you nothing but common courtesy." It may take several months for your brain to buy into these words, but when you do, it'll make it easier for you to deal with your former husband with basic respect and nothing more.

On the other end of the extreme, you have parents who are trying to "appear" to be friends with each other. The caution here is if you are over friendly, your child is confused about your relationship and may hold onto hope for reconciliation. Forcing your child to live in limbo prevents her from finding closure, moving forward, and healing.

While writing this book, I have prayed for guidance, wisdom, and humor to be available to me to share with you. I think sometimes we look at things too seriously and lose a perspective that can give us hope and inspiration. We wish you much success with your divorce and your life after divorce (AD), and we pray God will give you the courage, wisdom, and strength to do what is best for all involved.

CHAPTER 1

THE CAST OF CHARACTERS

Child

Throughout this book, when referring to a child, I'll be using the female references of she, her, etc., as it was a daughter who was a part of my divorce. I am hopeful that much of what is presented here is as relevant for "he" children as well.

Biological Father

The father of our child we'll call Rick, oh wait; that is his name, well we might as well use it. I am sure he is going to help me recall things of this shared experience, and will also shed light on his perspective of things (not that I am going to include much of what he contributes – only kidding).

Throughout this book, we will refer to Rick as our daughter's father or my former husband. I have a real issue with the term "ex-husband" so I might as well sidetrack right here and address this issue. According to the dictionary, "ex" is a prefix meaning "out of," "from," and hence "utterly," "thoroughly," and sometimes imparting a negative force or indicating a former title, status, etc. So I can see where it would apply, but the part of the definition which seems to have taken hold in our society is the "negative force" part. I just don't see why we need to add any more negative connotation to the process of divorce and the formerly married people involved in it. I also like the term "former" because it feels to me to be part of a continuum; we were once something (married), we have transitioned into something else (formerly married), and we will continue to have some type of relationship (parents). Let's face it people, you are going to have a relationship with this person; they're your child's other biological parent and no law, religious doctrine, or rebellious act on your part is going to change the simple fact.

Of course, I have some friends who refer to their former husband's as "sperm donors," and while the term is biologically correct, it somehow does not seem to play into any future relationship. I can't imagine going into a parent-teacher conference for my second grader and introducing ourselves as our daughter's "egg carrier" and "sperm donor." Speaking about second grade, see the "Weird Stories" section of this book.

Dad

We all know biological fathers may or may not turn into Dads, but my daughter was lucky enough to have a father (Rick) and a Dad (Boukie) – my "live-in significant other" (LISO) who shared her life since she was 2 ½ years old. I don't know when she started calling him Boukie, but it continues to be the name she uses for him.

Parental Unit

The "Parental Unit" as our daughter referred to us includes Rick, Boukie, and me. Sometimes we have been referred to as the "Unholy Trinity" (during the preteen angst years), and she has always said, "Why should I bother trying to play one of you against the other, you're all going to agree." See "Co-Parenting and Communication" to see how we achieved this consensus.

Our daughter was only 1 ½ years old when her parents divorced. I only mention that here to acknowledge that some suggestions that are presented in this book might be more difficult to implement with an older child.

CHAPTER 2

SETTING THE GROUND RULES

Suck It Up

I'm not going to assume you are going to like everything you read in this book; I can almost guarantee you won't. I can also tell you there are going to be several parts you read where the impulse to stick your finger down your throat is so strong that you will have to physically prevent yourself from doing so. However, the examples and scenarios I'm providing are true, so suck it up, take your finger out of your mouth, and keep reading.

Some suggestions in the book will have you glaring at me, saying, "No blasted way am I going to do that," (and yes I was being nice using the word blasted), but as the old adage goes, "Never say never." If your child's life were at stake, I can't think of anything that you wouldn't do to save her; well guess what, her life is at stake. Her emotional life is at stake; how she perceives herself, men, parents, women, confrontation, tough choices, and so much more are impacted by how you handle your divorce. So do what you have to do.

Your Divorce

This is YOUR divorce, not your child's. We often say things such as, "This is between Daddy and me, honey; it has nothing to do with you." Or, "We both love you so much, but sometimes adults just can't stay together, but we'll always be there for you because we love you."

BS – that's right, you heard me – BS. Telling a child a divorce has nothing to do with them is total BS. We know all children think the world revolves around them (or should). So any event, especially something as traumatic as a divorce, does have something to do with them. In fact, as far as they are concerned, it has everything to do with them. See chapter entitled, "It's All About Me" for more. The point here is your child didn't initiate this divorce so they shouldn't suffer its implementation.

Ground Rules

The grounds rules are:

Level the Playing Field

Stop, stop right now. Stop the negative interactions that you and your spouse shared; no name-calling, no intimidation, no threats, no withholding, nothing. As of this moment, those are gone. If you're not able to interact with each other in a civil manner, my first question is, "What are you, three years old?"

Now don't get mad. I know it's difficult to behave rationally when your emotional world is in upheaval, but you really do need to find a level playing field. If the two of you can't level the playing field on your own, seek help until you get your feet underneath you. As you'll hear many times throughout this book, I'm not an advocate of running to a lawyer when it comes to divorce. So when I say, "Seek help here," I'm suggesting an acquaintance both of you respect who is willing to work with you.

Mediator

This might sound bizarre, but if you have read this book to this point, bizarre things aren't surprising. The person I'm suggesting could be your postman, the dry cleaner, or even Uncle Tanocchi (you'll see him throughout the book). The job description for the person who helps you level the playing field is:

1. Someone you both respect,
2. A neutral party or someone you both feel could treat you neutrally,
3. Someone who doesn't have another agenda, and
4. Someone who has the time and willingness to walk through the fires of hell with the two of you.

I can't imagine someone willingly raising their hand, yelling "Pick me, pick me," when it comes time to find a mediator; however, mediators offer a great contribution to your needs. For the best results, the mutually agreed upon person you select shouldn't have another agenda. For example, as important to our spiritual lives as they are, a pastor (minister, priest, rabbi, etc.) has to have a religious agenda; it is a part of who they are and what they do. Therefore, it would be very difficult to disassociate themselves from their agenda. Another example might be your investment advisor who clearly doesn't want to see those assets divided and removed from his care. So, as long as you assure your dry cleaner you both will continue to take your clothes there, you have at least mitigated his most obvious agenda.

A mediator also has to be someone who is willing to see several sides of the same story; after all, there are always at least three sides, yours, mine, and the truth. The mediator must be able to help you explore all those sides and articulate options or different perspectives.

A mediator has to be tough, a thick-skinned person who's not going to take your setbacks personally. He/she has to be able to ask tough questions, be consistent about demanding you treat each other with respect, keep the progress moving forward, and know when to end a session. While doing all of this, you don't want your mediator to be the "fixer." The issues (and there are a whole ton of issues) are between you and your spouse, so it is you and your spouse who have to fix them.

If you find yourselves in need of a professional, I would have to say a good mediator is worth every penny you pay. Be sure to do your homework, find the right person for both of you, and understand the obligations you both have in this process—not only financial obligations, but personal and emotional energies as well.

Once the two of you are on the same page with the shared goal of getting through this divorce in a manner that is not harmful to your child, you can then move to the next step. Rick and I were able to start with and maintain a level playing field, which meant we didn't have to seek a mediator until our plans were complete. (See the "Parenting Plan" in Appendix A for more.)

Avoid Sides

Trying to get his friends to see your point of view, or your friends to ignore your former spouse, are actions that are a waste of time and energy. And just in case you haven't gotten clued in on it yet, getting through a divorce takes a lot of time and energy; there is no need to waste it on actions that aren't constructive. Its human nature to want to take sides, and it might actually make you feel good to hear someone berating your former husband and extolling all of your wonderful virtues. However, at the end of the day, what did you achieve? And let's face it; do you really need another person to identify some things you don't like about your former husband? Come on, your list is big enough on its own.

Be Civil to In-Laws

Well, at least as much as you were when you were married; remember you are divorcing the father of your child, not the aunts/uncles, cousins, and grandparents. Your child is connected to "that side of the family" and will be for the remainder of her life. Now I'm not saying you have to go for coffee with your former mother-in-law, but you do want to support your child's ongoing relationship with her father's family.

Here's a quick weird story about family connections. Before our daughter was born, Rick's brother had a daughter and on the first day of school each year, Rick and I would show up at their house with an apple and wish her luck at school. When we got divorced, this niece was about 9 years old. Rick and I discussed it, and we agreed to show up at her house on her first day of school. To acknowledge it was a bit weird or awkward, we gave her a pear instead of an apple.

While the story is cute and true, I can't promise you that maintaining a relationship with your in-laws after a divorce is easy. I can promise you it'll take an effort on your part. This effort may be one you frankly don't want to make; especially if you had a difficult time getting along with them when you were married. (Did I say that out loud?). But you will do what you need to do to ensure your child can enjoy an extended family who brings depth and variety to her life experiences.

CHAPTER 3

OUR DIVORCE

Remember planning your wedding? Whether you had some elaborate affair orchestrated by a wedding planner or a small gathering in your backyard with close friends and family, you had to plan your wedding. Even if you hopped a plane and headed to Vegas because everyone wants to get married by an Elvis impersonator; you still had to plan.

For some of us, trying to accommodate the varied needs of our mother, mother-in-law, and bridesmaids seemed to take more time and attention than meeting the needs of ourselves or our husbands, but try you did. You struggled with what you should get for wedding favors, where Uncle Tanocchi should sit at the reception, and even what song to play as your first song as husband and wife.

Those decisions were not nearly as important as how you are going to protect and guide your child(ren) through the process of your divorce. You need to plan your divorce with as much or more of a commitment than you gave to the wedding. Rick and I elected to avoid attorneys (we highly recommend that) and create a parenting plan. We wanted a plan we could live with and one we felt would guide us as we moved past the divorce throughout the rest of our daughter's life.

The best part about planning your divorce is it starts you on the road to communicating with someone who you actually never want to speak to again. In fact, you might rather stick this person with a sharp object or fantasize the painful removal of a body part (and we all know which one I am talking about), but instead you have to talk with each other and work as a team to create a plan to move forward with your most precious possession, your child(ren).

See Appendix A for a more comprehensive list of ideas about parenting plans, but here are some helpful hints:

- For every decision you make, be sure it responds positively to the question, "Is this the best choice for our child(ren)?"
- Don't take things personally; you don't have to win every discussion point.
- Divide your thinking into categories: school, health, dental care, college, sports, summer activities, insurance, visiting schedules, purchasing a car, prom and specialty clothing, school club fees, clothing allotments, and any other possibility that may arise.

It's better to over plan than to create a plan full of gaps.

- Look at each category and decide what issues (time, money, who drives, etc.) need to be addressed.

- Talk to parents with older kids who have already gone through this process to see if they can provide any additional insights or issues that you haven't thought of.

- Decide how you want to resolve differences (because you are definitely going to have them). For example, if you don't want to donate to the purchase of a new car, you can compromise, agree to allocate a set amount of money, or agree to purchase a used car. If you agree to disagree, that's fine, but make sure that it is clearly explained in the plan.

- After you have muddled through these discussions, write everything down and start a preliminary plan. The plan can be as detailed as you want. Especially with this preliminary plan, it's important not to leave anything out. You are going to revisit this plan several times before you bring it to the mediator, so more is better now. You can cut things out, rearrange, modify, and edit it along the way, but you certainly do not want to forget or overlook something.

Bring the plan to:

- Someone who has had personal experience in putting together a successful parenting plan, or

- The person you sought out to be your "level the playing field" resource, or
- A child psychologist, or
- You thought I was going to say Uncle Tanocchi didn't you? Well, it may be him, or
- The mediator; in our case, the mediator also served as our joint attorney during the divorce proceedings.

Don't rush; take your time. Never make a decision if you are feeling fearful, angry, or hateful. This document is going to be your blueprint for the remainder of your child's life. Treat it carefully and honor it.

Our Court Proceedings

I warned you about things getting a bit weird, but open your minds and hearts to see if you can get any lessons from these next experiences. Rick and I spent a great deal of time going through a parenting plan, anticipating as much as we could, and putting a process in place to deal with future issues. Next, we met with the mediator and reviewed everything. Now this is 1994 and the concept of a parenting plan was not really recognized yet. So the mediator had to fill out the standard divorce papers and give them to the judge along with our parenting plan.

Note: Since I started writing this book, several sources have created parenting plans and some states have passed legislation requiring a parenting plan as part of the divorce proceeding. Your mediator/attorney should be able to point you in the direction of resources. Or simply do a web search for parenting plans and explore options to decide which one makes sense for the two of you.

On the day of our hearing before the judge, Rick and I stroll into the courtroom, arm in arm, and proceed to sit at the same table. The judge looks at us over his glasses and says, "One of you is supposed to sit at the other table."

We both start to get up and Rick says, "Ladies first," so I move over to the other table while the judge sits with a perplexed look on his face.

The judge proceeds to ask for some documentation we brought with us. No offense Rick, but keeping organized files was always my area of expertise. So while Rick is trying to flip through our folder, I lean over and tell him where to find the information the judge is asking for. He says, "Thanks," and then gives the judge the documents.

Well this pattern repeats itself a couple of more times until the judge says to me, "Do you just want to go over there and sit with him?"

I thought he was serious, so I said, "Sure," and went over to the other table while the judge shook his head.

We got through all the questions, answers, and documentation as pleasantly as if we were ordering lunch in a fancy restaurant. Then the judge asks, "Are you two sure you want to get a divorce?"

We turn to look at each other, smile, and in one voice say, "Absolutely."

Needless to say, when the proceedings were over and our nominal court's fees paid, we then turned and strolled out, arm in arm.

The Divorce Celebration

So you might have chuckled at our courtroom behavior, but now you're going to totally flip out. We left the courtroom, picked up our daughter who was staying with Rick's brother, got back into the car, and proceeded to drive five hours to spend the weekend with our friends. Yes, you heard me correctly; Rick, me, and our daughter spent the weekend with friends to share a divorce celebration, so to speak.

Rick and I had been together for 13 years, so we talked a lot about the good times we shared, and then we talked about the events leading up to our divorce. We didn't do this in a judgmental way, but rather as a way to reaffirm our decision to get divorced. We congratulated each other on how hard we worked on the parenting plan. We recommitted to implementing the plan to the best of our abilities. Then, we wished each other future love and happiness. I know some of you reading are hoping we had a bon voyage boff, but we didn't (you remember where that got me the last time).

Ok, some of you have tissues catching tears leaking out of your eyes; some of you have your fingers approaching the gag reflex in your throat, and some of you are boldly stating that I am full of BS. Well, first of all, this is what happened. Secondly, what is really so weird about it?

Let's say you work for a software development company (as a freelance technical writer, I have much experience there), and you've created a new software product. After launching the product, you find it doesn't work as you intended. So you have a meeting and you talk about all the good things about the product, the bad things, and the steps you took that were off track. You might even congratulate the team for delivering the product, even though it wasn't successful, you would then recommit to correcting the software and working hard to launch a better solution. Finally, you would wish each member of the team future success (again, no boffing). So what is so different from this process than what we went through at our divorce celebration?

Now you are probably saying, "Well one of these things was more important than the other; they're not the same at all, one is work and one is your life." Well, many of you believe your work is your life. (If you are one of those, immediately go to the "Heal Yourself" section in the book.) Others of you are saying you are not as emotionally involved at work as you are in your marriage, and you would be right. I guess my point is you want to take every chance you are given to remove the emotional baggage that can negatively influence your common sense and good judgment. You want to attempt to make your important decisions under the best circumstances.

CHAPTER 4

CO-PARENTING AND COMMUNICATIONS

For the rest of your child's life, both parents are going to communicate. Say it, say it again, say it like you mean it, and say it like it won't be the most painful thing you have to do.

Find Ways to Communicate

Rick and I were fortunate in one regard when we divorced because our daughter was only 1 ½ years old. We had agreed to split the week taking care of her until she went to daycare or school. So every few days, whoever had our child would take her over to the other parent's house. During the exchange, we would discuss all the very important aspects of an infant's life, such as feeding, bowel movements, sleeping, and baby necessities.

It was similar to going to the auto mechanic and giving him an update on your vehicle before you had him change the oil—no emotion, just the facts, which made it very comfortable.

However, for us, there was an added bonus. The house where I was living had a safe neighborhood and a nice yard so building snowmen, planting seeds in the garden, playing with the dog, and using the swing set were always done at my house even if it was a "Dad" day.

Of course because our child was just the most precious and adorable infant ever to live, we also got to share the "what she did recently" show and tell of parenting—spitting out peas, making funny faces, glowering at you when you tried to sneak those peas in another time, walking, talking, and so much more. So not only was it comfortable, it was also enjoyable.

Because of this, our communications got off to a great start, and coupled with our communication commitment in our parenting plan, we were well underway. In the early years, we spoke by phone once a week or so and still spent a lot of time sharing the "what she did recently" show and tell.

Over the years, we maintained weekly phone calls. Our daughter is now 21 years old, and as I write this book, Rick and I don't speak weekly, but I would say we have at least quarterly check-ins and "as needed" phone calls. It doesn't have to be a nightmare to communicate with your co-parent. Especially in today's high-tech world, you can email, IM, text, leave voicemail, or any other number of other methods. Create a communication that works for you and take deep breaths before and after your talks; it really does work.

Keep Each Other Informed

While it's easy to hide some details by sharing only the cute stories, it's important to keep each other informed about any troublesome matters. Boukie, my daughter, and I moved out of state when she was 3 ½ so the commitment to keep Rick informed grew even stronger. Don't worry, Rick and his daughter still spent a lot of time together; see "Weird Stories" for details.

Over the years, we have made sure to give each other our impressions of just about every aspect of our daughter's life. Do you think she is putting too much pressure on herself at school? Does she have good friends? How does she like living where we are now? How much does she talk about missing Rick in between visits? What are the happy things she talks about? What are the sad things she talks about? How were her visits to her grandparents' houses?

From this list, you can see we could've gotten into very defensive conversations or spent hours justifying one feeling or another, but we had agreed from the start to share this information as FYI—no judgment, no finger pointing. If we thought there was an area of concern we should do something about, we kicked around ideas and came up with a plan. By keeping this level of communication, neither parent was caught off guard or confused about anything going on in our daughter's life. Pretty cool, wouldn't you say? I fear that many married couples probably don't have this level of communication about their children; hmm, what does that mean? I'll have to think about it and get back to you.

It's easy to keep each other informed and share information if you keep the judgment out of the equation.

Commiserate

Maybe this paragraph should fall into the "Weird Stories" section because it is a bit weird that former spouses, now co-parents, would spend time commiserating with each other, but the venting was good for both of us. We got insights into how we were feeling as parents, how we were feeling about our daughter (and if truth be told it's not always with sunshine and light), how we were feeling about the other parent's parenting behaviors, and so much more.

All right, I will admit sometimes when Rick was whining about some thing or another in his life, I may have rolled my eyes, maybe once, maybe twice, but no more. However, I'm sure he would admit to the same thing. But hey, at least we still tried.

Agree to Disagree

As you will see in Appendix A, the parenting plan does include a strategy for dealing with disagreement. For Rick and me, the plan was:

1. Discuss it, throw out ideas, see if we could come up with something; if that failed

2. Contact our mediator and work with her to see if she could help us resolve the matter; if that failed,

3. Take the matter to a child psychologist to see if he/she could help; if that failed

4. Take the matter back to court.

Fortunately, we never even had to go to step 2 (although one time it was close), but the point here is you have to be willing to discuss tough topics, collaborate on resolutions, and even "give in" (agree to disagree) on some strategies. If this scenario occurs, I suggest you implement the strategy for a short period of time and report back success or failure (honestly) to the other parent. Eek, that might mean even more communication, but by this point, you should be doing pretty well with that.

Make Joint Decisions

Whenever possible, make joint decisions. I'm not saying that you have to call the other spouse from the department store, take a picture on your cell phone of the Easter dress you are thinking of buying her, text it to him, and then stand around and wait for his vote. However, that's not truly a horrible idea. But what I am saying is that bigger decisions should be made after sharing a conversation about it. Things like, is she too young for braces, should she play soccer or softball this season; which summer camp do you think she would like better, are all topics that would benefit from a shared discussion with your co-parent.

If money is involved in the decision, you definitely need to give the other parent a voice.

Handling Confrontations

If someone knew the best way to handle confrontation, there would be no wars, no gangs, and no enemies. While we don't have a clear roadmap for handling confrontations, here are a few suggestions.

1. Be clear about the issue you want to resolve.
2. Seek understanding first.
3. Be sure you do not have a hidden agenda.
4. Define your intentions and keep the focus on your child.
5. Focus on the issue, not on the people involved.
6. Focus on solutions, not causes of the problem.
7. Schedule a discussion as soon as is mutually convenient for both people; don't let things fester.
8. Ensure that both people have uninterrupted time and space for the discussion.
9. Behave during the discussion as if you were having a business meeting.
10. Ask for help when you need it, sometimes a person with no vested interest can set the stage for a more effective meeting.
11. Avoid emotional statements and blaming.
12. Write down the solution you both reach, who is responsible for each part, and how you will measure success. Send it to the other parent in an email to avoid misunderstanding.
13. Be open to re-evaluate the solution to see if an even better idea arises.

Realize that most things do not have to be set in stone, reach a tentative agreement, implement it, and then re-evaluate it.

CHAPTER 5

SINCE THEN –
LIFE AFTER DIVORCE

As I mentioned, right after the divorce, Rick and I lived in close proximity to each other for about a year and sharing our parenting responsibilities was logistically rather easy to accomplish. When we moved, things required a bit more thought, time, and expense. We decided our child would call each grandparent on alternating Sundays; at the time, the phone company had a 5-cent Sunday plan so a five-minute call only cost a quarter. What we didn't realize was a three – and four-year-old girl could tell her grandparents quite a bit of information in a voice so animated and fast that we ended up spending as much money translating what she had said to them in the first place. Still, it was a joyous experience for everyone (and a precursor to explaining the concept of money to our toddler).

We would also visit every month; one month Rick would fly to our home, the next our daughter and I would fly to his home. This was an outrageously expensive plan in just airfare alone, but we continued to do this until Rick moved closer to where we lived. Once he moved, the commute could be accomplished by a four-hour car ride, so we took turns driving every month.

With all of this commuting we did try to accommodate each other as much as possible. We would stay in each other's houses when we would traipse over the countryside to see our daughter. That's right, when Rick came to our house, he would stay in the guest room. There is nothing freakier than waking up, heading toward the bathroom for your morning constitutional, and seeing your former husband walking out the door across the hall, but we continued with this arrangement for over 12 years.

Every month, Rick would spend a weekend with his daughter. As she got older and got involved in more school and community activities, it got to the point where Rick would come here versus us traveling to his house. So there were times the Parental Unit was all in attendance at school activities, sports events, or even serving as multiple hosts for her birthday parties. There were other times when the Parental Unit was the Easter Bunny, Santa, or the Tooth Fairy. While our neighbors would shake their heads, chuckle to themselves, and even mutter remarks, they got used to us. But that never mattered anyway; we were all child-focused.

As our daughter entered her teen years, her availability for monthly visits slightly diminished but I think Rick and I can proudly say we still ensured they visited at least every two months. Since our daughter started college in Chicago and then Paris, France, our monthly visits had dropped off dramatically, but whenever she returned home, Rick was welcome here (welcomed is a better term than endured, right?)

Do Unto Others

If your child came home from school and starting telling you all of these ugly things about another student, you would stop her and ask what happened at school to make her say these ugly things. You might also throw out some well-worn adages, such as "If you can't say something nice, don't say anything at all." Even when you found out the child in question did something mean to your child, you would spend time with your child, helping them explore their feelings and helping them to understand why saying ugly things about another person not only does not resolve anything, but makes you feel bad as well.

HELLO, please look in the mirror and remind yourself of this exchange the next time something ugly comes streaming out of your mouth about your co-parent.

Trash Talk

The first rule in this section is never trash talk about the other parent, and I mean NEVER in any form where your child could hear. Ok, your child is in bed, has been asleep for hours, and you are enjoying a glass of wine (or three) and your best friend calls and asks how your daughter's last visit with her father went, and ... well, there is no way your child could ever hear you. So you unload on your friend until her ears are burning and the bottle of wine is empty. Do you feel better? Well in some regards you do (minus the hangover of course), but what did you achieve? A few moments of feeling you've been heard, that you've been vindicated in your belief about your former spouse, so was it worth it? Hell yes, but that's where it needs to begin and where it needs to end.

No subtle innuendos about the other parent as you are having a phone conversation with Uncle Tanocchi (I missed him so I had to bring him back). No references while you are preparing breakfast about how much her father hates French Toast, even though it is your child's favorite. No subtle facial expressions when caller ID shows said parent is calling. All of these behaviors have to go because, as we all know, our children are brilliant and perceptive, and they will pick up on these things.

Rick and I were so successful with out commitment to never talk trash about the other person that when our daughter was 7 years old, we had to try to explain to her why we got along so well, spoke kindly about each other, but couldn't be married. So while that brilliant and perceptive child made us aware of how well we were doing with this commitment, we also realized we could tone down our positive statements about each other.

At this writing, our daughter is 21 and she could not count on one hand the number of times either of her parents had ever said something even remotely trashy about the other parent, so far so good! Just think we'll probably both walk her down the aisle when she gets married, smiling, and chit chatting like life-long friends. (By this time, you are probably not surprised by this statement – good for you!)

"My Father" Stories

Similar to trash talk and the cause of my tongue being nearly bitten to pieces innumerable times is the next rule—earnestly listen to and appropriately respond to "My Father" stories. These are the stories your child tells you after having spent time with her father. Whether it was just a weekend together or an extended stay, your child is going to come home with these terrific My Father stories. Trust me, you are going to have to smile, suck it up, bite your tongue, and after she is in slumber land, grab the bottle of wine. "My Father and I went to the zoo, and then My Father helped me actually pet a goat, and then My Father bought me a big bag of popcorn, and then My Father…" (by which point, you are gritting your teeth or maybe your eyes have glazed over, but you need to keep listening).

By the end of the description of the "My Father day," you have come to realize he never gave her the required nap, did not provide any fruits or vegetables in her diet, and never refused her request even ONCE. Instead of going off on this wired-out, sugar-high, glowing child, you have to say, "Wow, it sure sounds like you and your father had a great day." Of course you are saying this as you are trying to get her to finish her dinner with some actual nutrients, and then head her into the bath because she smells like the goat she petted, and then rock her to sleep because geez she cannot fall asleep on her own for SOME STRANGE REASON. Deep breath, hang in there.

Support the Wonderful Things

As you know, Rick comes to our home on a regular basis. While there are several strange aspects to the arrangement, there were also some side benefits we never anticipated. For example, I am domestically challenged; the truth of the matter is I can do any or all of it, but frankly, I don't LIKE doing it. So when it came time to teach our daughter how to cook, how to bake, how to knit, how to plant flowers, and how to create symmetrical art projects, in stepped Rick.

Now I am not trash talking myself here because in preparation for their cooking and baking times, I taught her how to prepare a meal schedule, generate a grocery list of nutritional items, and clip coupons. So you've got the ying to the yang, and as a result, she is able to create and prepare quite tasty treats. Regrettably, her father never did teach her the fine art of cleaning up after herself in the kitchen, but since our family rule had always been, "If I cook, you clean," I guess he never felt the need.

Art projects, science projects, and all of those time-consuming projects which always seemed to require the tiniest components needing to be glued, fitted, adhered, or somehow put together by someone with far more patience than I possessed were shared joyfully with Rick. My praise was genuine and appreciative.

Do NOT Fix It

Here is a tricky area, especially if you are a fixer like I used to be (notice I am encouraging myself by saying "used to be"). When your child has a separate relationship with the other parent, there are going to be times when she expresses concern about a particular event or comment the other parent made and then wants to discuss it with you.

Ugh, rock and hard place, rock and hard place, Houston, we have a problem. Your desire is to help your child explore things she doesn't understand, but (and it is a BIG but), you need to do so without breaking any of the other rules of trash talking or berating the other parent. And probably most importantly, you need to keep in mind you want to help your child learn how to explore and understand the process of dealing with new experiences.

Now might be the best time to put on your "Shrink Hat." You know the perception you have of going to a psychologist with a huge box of tissues, your broken heart on your sleeve, and the person says, "So how does that make you feel?" Well, even though this may not be the type of response you wanted, it does do several positive things for you:

1. It allows you to vent,
2. It acknowledges your venting,
3. It allows you to explore your feelings, and
4. It keeps the resolution of the problem where it belongs—with you.

So get the tissues and your calm demeanor ready and help your child to explore the situation, event, or comment. Simply pose questions, give encouraging grunts, nod your head, listen attentively, hug, and retrieve the next box of tissues if necessary. You can assure her that you have confidence in her ability to work things out. You may also want to provide her with some venting options like punching a pillow, doing cartwheels until you get dizzy, or the time-honored tradition of a bowl of ice cream. However, whatever you do, let your child know you are more than willing to revisit this with her. This tells her that she always has someone she can turn to when she needs to.

CHAPTER 6

IT'S ALL ABOUT ME

As you know, your child's focus is on herself, but even with all of this self-attention, a child is often too young or has not shared enough experiences with life to understand everything going on around her. (Hmm, I still feel that way sometimes). So it's important to touch base and spend time talking with her not only during the difficult times but on a regular basis. Setting a foundation of talking to your child regularly will make talking to her as a teen and young adult much easier (at least it has for us).

There are tons of books written by far more qualified professionals to help you with this, but here is a cute story that focuses on one aspect of communication. My aunt (who at the time was in her late 60's) was driving her seven-year-old grandson to a sporting event. Buckled into the backseat of her car, he was busy exploring his new wallet. Then he asks, "Grammy, what is sex?"

Kudos to my aunt for not spinning the car out of control as she undertook this question. Raised Italian Catholic, my aunt then proceeded to go into a monologue about love and marriage (in that specific order), the various ways married people can express their love for each other, how sex is just another form of expression (geared specifically for having children), and how people should not engage in sex without being married (ah, she made the church proud). Then she said, "Why do you ask?"

And he said, "Well, there is a card in my new wallet where it asks for your name, address, and sex.

Moral: always clarify what your child is asking. Not only will you be better able to respond to her, but you may not have to put yourself in the uncomfortable position of answering one of those "tricky" questions.

Answer Their Questions

All children have questions especially when they are encountering something they don't understand or they're uncomfortable with. In the case of a divorce, you can be assured your child does not understand what is going and certainly doesn't like it. Therefore, it's important to make yourself available to your child so she can explore her questions and concerns. Now I realize this is not always easy, but you do need to make the effort.

When I was growing up, there were four children, each two years apart. My mother worked outside of the home, and she was involved in so many volunteer activities that she was voted "Women of the Year" in our community not once, not twice, but on three different occasions. She was involved with community sports, Red Cross, Boy and Girl Scouts, the volunteer fire department, and the list goes on and on. I'm giving you this background so you can understand that when she interfaced with an inquisitive child (yes, me), she would often respond to my questions with, "Because I said so."

When I became a parent, I vowed I would never say that to my child. Well, I kept the promise until she turned 18. After an extended conversation about a topic I believed should have had no discussion at all (body part piercing), I finally said, "Well my dear, my final vote is no and the reason is BISS." While she wasn't happy with my response, she did end up laughing because while I didn't break my promise to never say, "Because I said so" she got the message that I was at my wit's end.

God did decide to bless me with one of the most inquisitive children ever (aka NOSY). But we need to give our children an avenue to communicate, to express their feelings, and to vent. Remember the "moral" of the sex story above as you attempt to provide answers to your child; in fact, it might be a good idea to start every answer with either, "What do you think?" or "Can you ask me that in a different way so I can be sure I understand your question?" You might save a lot of time and explanation.

Giving Them a Place to Vent

As our daughter got older and began to explore her feelings further, I realized there were times she needed to vent. Keep in mind she lived with me full-time, spent a weekend a month with her father and sometimes a week here or there with him as well. After a "My Father" weekend, there were times she was short-tempered with me or just plain old crabby. So I thought of an idea of giving her a "safe" place. I told her whenever she and I were in her bed, with the sheet pulled up over our heads, she was able to say anything she wanted and she wouldn't get into trouble and she wouldn't hurt anyone's feelings.

Inside the safe zone, there were NO ramifications for the things she said. In fact, while in the zone, I didn't even offer advice or my opinions. What I did was allow her to talk and I would listen, then I would say back what she said, ask questions to help guide her to resolve these feelings, and then tell her I loved her and would support her. This strategy gives the child the impression she is in control, she has a say in how she reacts to things, and it helps set the stage for her decision-making skills.

At first, she was quite skeptical about this arrangement and tentatively started with, "I miss my dad after he goes back home."

When I replied, "I know you miss him honey, and I bet he misses you too," you could tell she was surprised when I said that with a smile on my face and a big hug for her. She was probably expecting me to get upset because she may have thought she was not supposed to miss him when she was with me. She was pleased to get a supportive response.

At first, I would be the one who would have to ask, "Do you think you need to go to our safe place and talk for awhile?" Of course, this was at times when she was being so out of sorts that I actually went to the Yellow Pages to see if they had a

"Rent an Aunt" listing where I could pawn the kid off for a couple of hours (wouldn't that be a great idea?)

As time went on, however, she would invite me to join her, and we would talk about a lot of different things. I have to say I got a great deal of reconnaissance about her feelings toward her parental unit from which I truly benefitted, and she got a place where she could vent. We always ended our time under the "dome of safety" with a tickle, laugh, and a hug.

I also received a wonderful additional benefit to this arrangement I didn't expect at the time I created this "safe zone." As my daughter grew into pre-teen and teen years, we were able to use the "Cover All" to discuss things about school, friends, boys, and other topics most children that age would never discuss with their parents. It has given us a vehicle to communicate honestly and to be closer as she moved towards adulthood. (Wait, what did I just say? How could my infant who I just gave birth to yesterday be an adult today?)

About Truth

A room full of people could spend hours, days, and weeks talking about truth and never get a consensus on it or how to divulge it. We wanted our daughter to know that one of the things wonderful about truth is you never have to worry about it being untrue. I know this may sound weird; but by this point, you're probably used to weird. You all know what I am talking about when you tell a fib; you have to remember it was a fib for the rest of your life. I, for one, don' have the extra storage compartment in my brain to remember fibs so I'm just better off with the truth.

Let's look at an example. You fib and tell your friend you had to work late when in actuality you went with another friend to a movie. Your friend calls the next day to see how the extra hours of work went. Now what do you do? Fib again. Then several weeks later, in a conversation with this friend, she mentions a movie she wants to see and, without thinking, you blurt out, "I've already seen it; it was great; you'll love it." She inquires, "When did you see it?" and the entire circle of fibbing or getting caught in your previous fib continues.

I just can't deal with the drama it can cause. If I think my speaking the truth is going to hurt someone's feelings, I usually start with, "Well, this is not intended to hurt your feelings but I think..." Of course, when you start a sentence with such an introduction, the person is immediately defensive, so that is another issue you have to deal with. However, I would rather deal with explaining myself instead of storing fibs.

Because of our commitment to truth, our daughter had difficulty with some aspects of truth, and she thought her Parental Unit was being mean to her at times. She might ask, "How do I look?" (She is dressed in three different seasonal attires, in a multitude of colors which will never coordinate, and her hair hasn't seen a brush in weeks.) Her response from Boukie was a grunted, "Silly."

From me she got, "Well how do you feel about what you have on?" She would grimace to Boukie's response and roll her eyes to mine.

But what we were trying to help her understand is when you have truth, you always have a security in knowing it will always be the truth. You may not always like what we say, you may think we are being ugly, but no matter what else you think, you will know, without a moment's doubt, that it is the truth. There's a great deal of security and comfort in those feelings, and now as she has gotten older, she seems to grasp the blessing in uncensored truth.

Let Your Child See You

While this chapter is all about the child, part of the focus has to be about enabling your child to see who you are too. In addition to being her mother, I've always tried to have my daughter see me as a professional woman, an aromatherapist (fill in your own hobby here), a spouse (or equivalent), a best friend, and a person who loves dancing. I wanted her to understand that while I loved being her mother (and still do), I was also a lot of other things, and those things required some of my time, energy, attention, and focus.

I also let her see me cry (often over sappy movies), hear me laugh (way too loud), see me ignore her when I was in the middle of a writing assignment (not well received by her, but oh well), and do all of the embarrassing things parents are prone to do.

What I tried to not let her see, until she was much older, was any of my frustration or disappointment in her father, other family members, or relatives. She was not surprised when I invited every person who was ever in her life to her high school graduation; she actually thought I was looking forward to seeing most of these people. When the day was over and I had my aching feet up on a chair, a glass of wine in my hand (well, ok, it was a bottle), and a cheerful wave goodbye to the final guests, she actually was surprised I was thrilled they were all leaving.

CHAPTER 7

HEAL YOURSELF

No matter how much you read about participating in a "healthy" divorce or how much desire you have to make sure you don't put your child into a situation which is neither healthy nor her fault, you will not be truly successful in your efforts unless you heal yourself.

Go to the self-help section of any bookstore; you could spend weeks, if not months, reading all of the information available to you about helping yourself. I went into a bookstore recently just to confirm this, and wow, I was overwhelmed. Some of these materials are based on solid research and offer practical suggestions. Others are, well, as my mother used to say, "interesting" (and you know what that means). I guess what I am saying is should you feel the need for help; there is an abundance of materials to assist you. However, to succeed, you need to do the work.

The good news is the work you'll be doing is for your benefit as well as your child's wellbeing. Here are a couple of things I did to heal after my divorce. I have been fortunate enough to incorporate them into my daily living ever since and I am a much happier and healthier woman for the effort.

Laugh

During times of change, stress, turmoil, or even just during the hectic schedules of our everyday lives, we get caught up. So what can we do while we're hustling and bustling through life? You got it, we can laugh.

I won't go into the scientific research indicating all of the benefits of laughter. I won't start on the beauty secrets which explain how many muscles we use when we laugh. I won't even discuss the spiritual benefits of laughter on the soul. Let's get funny about it. You are in the grocery store doing the same old, same old and trying to get it done as quickly as possible. All of a sudden you hear laughter a few aisles over; you can't help but be slightly distracted and feel a twinkle building in your heart. The laughter goes on and on and before you know it, you're laughing too and you have no idea why. So okay, during this fit of laughter, instead of picking up the fat free, cholesterol free, no sodium, no flavor item on your list, you end up buying the yummy and decadent item. That's okay because when you get home and take it out of the bag and realize what you did, you have yet another excuse to start laughing again.

And if you think laughing in the grocery store is fun, you should try it in the post office. The lines are ALWAYS long and half of the employees put up their "next window please" sign as the lines get longer and longer; that's a really good place. Of course, you want to pretend to be reading something in the magazine you're holding so the other people in line don't think you are crazy. See didn't that thought just lift your spirits a little? Go ahead, take some time right now, think of other places where laughter would really be hysterical, and oh yeah, laugh about it.

P.S. The Motor Vehicle Department is a really good place. Inside a church is not a good place and neither are libraries, but those are only a couple of places which don't qualify. There are tons of places where a good laugh is just what the doctor ordered. (Hey wait, how about the doctor's office?)

Prioritize

You are mother, housecleaner, professional woman, confidante, family nutritionist, short-order cook, cab driver, classroom volunteer, nurse, scheduler, baker, friend, and the list goes on. (In fact, I thought if I continued the list, I would get exhausted just looking at it.) Obviously, you need to prioritize what has to happen when.

Keep a Schedule – As a freelance writer with several clients (as well as all of those things in the paragraph before), I could NOT keep anything straight without my calendar. Now, some people think taking the time to create a calendar requires more time than they have, but I can assure you it saves time in the long run. Some people think my living by a calendar is too rigid, but I do allow for modifications, adjustments, and a couple of minutes here and there to do some sun salutations (yoga), smell my own daffodils (yes, I planted them myself), or have a quick chat with a friend.

Eat a Frog – I always tell people, "If you eat a frog, nothing else can taste so bad (of course, this was before I tried escargot), but the point is, put the thing you least want to do at the top of your list so you can get it done and over with. You'll waste more time, energy, and emotion if you keep something hanging over your head.

Be Selfish – You weren't expecting that one were you? Here is the problem, according to dictionary.com selfish means "devoted to or caring only for oneself; concerned primarily with one's own interests, benefits, welfare, etc., regardless of others." While I have no intention of rewriting the dictionary; I am going to rewrite this entry. I believe selfish should mean "devoted to or caring for oneself, concerned first with one's own welfare." By simply removing a couple of words, we turn this word from being a narcissistic word into one which can be related to prioritization.

You HAVE to take care of yourself because:

- No one else is going to,
- If you are depleted of energy, you could get ill, and then who can you take care of,

- If you are depleted of emotional energy, you are going to be a "you know what" to others around you, and the list goes on.

You must take care of yourself so you have the strength, focus, and life-loving appreciation to take care of others too.

What Is Important?

You might think this question belongs in the "Prioritize" section. It does to a certain extent, but what I want to talk about here is evaluating things to determine what part of your attention they deserve. Here are a couple of steps you can take to achieve success in this area:

Can you control it? – When something happens, ask yourself, "Can I control this?" If the answer is NO, well then let it go. I know it's easier said than done. I've been trying to make it easier with each attempt (sometimes I succeed), but whether I succeed or not, I still ask myself the question. If the answer is no, then I work to let it go.

Let's look at this a little closer so you don't think I'm out of my mind. Let's say you're going on a business trip and your flight is delayed. Can you control this? No. So what can you do? Calmly check your options for the quickest departure, then contact your business associates to inform them of the delay and THAT'S IT. Everyone understands flight delays are out of our control. So frantically trying to find another flight, calling every business contact you have to see if they have any ideas on getting the plane to leave, or rushing to the customer service counter every three minutes to check the status of the flight are all things you did because why? Get it? These were all time wasters, energy wasters, and emotionally draining, worthless actions.

So the next time something like this happens, after doing the responsible thing, get a cup of tea, open your notebook and write an "atta girl" note to yourself for handling this situation better. Then write a love note to your child detailing something about her you really enjoy.

Can you influence it? – I know it sounds similar to the first one; but in this case, maybe there is an area of influence which would then require you to take a couple of steps before it falls into the "not in my control" category. Let's say you're heading to the dry cleaners and the car in front of you gets hit by another car coming through the intersection. Can you control that? No. Can you influence the outcome? Yes, you can call 911 and provide the location of the accident.

Using this example of an area you can influence, you can then go back to the original topic of what is really important? If you believe the situation is not as important as something else that requires your attention, then let it go, drive away, and get on with what you were doing.

Create a plan – When something falls into the categories of being something you can control, influence, and is important to you, then create a plan to deal with it. As a writer and project manager, I could write an entire book on planning (hmmm, note to self). But here are the basics:

1. Start with goals,
2. Develop objectives to meet each goal,
3. Be sure the objectives are measurable so you can see your success and create workarounds for your failures,
4. Consider the resources you need for your plan,
5. Establish a timeframe for the plan, and
6. Implement.

You Have the Power

I know right now you are feeling overwhelmed and maybe even powerless, but you have to continuously support the notion that you do, in fact, have the power. This power comes from the premise that you always have the power of choice. You cannot choose some of the things you encounter during a day or how someone is going to treat you, but you can always choose how you are going to respond, behave, and move forward.

It may not seem like a lot of power because it may not influence things to go the way you want them to, but it is a solid power no one can take away from you. Do you hear me? No one can take this power away from you—how powerful is that? What can happen, however, is you can give your power away, and it's really quite easy to do. As soon as you let someone else make a decision for you, you have given your power away. DON'T DO IT!

There were days during the divorce process when I felt totally overwhelmed. We were living in a very old house that was so drafty it would take an entire cord of wood to keep the place warm each month. As a freelance writer, I was having trouble getting a writing assignment which would allow me to take care of my infant, so money was tight. "Friends" were calling to provide support (aka tell me what to do regarding the divorce), and my family was suffocating me with suggestions. Since running away from home was not an option, I would walk around the house (putting up sheets over the drafty windows) repeating incessantly, "I have the power, I have the power, I get to decide, I will not give my power away, I have the power." Talk about a mantra, I'm surprised my daughter's first words weren't "I've got the power" because she heard it so many times.

When I finally incorporated the mantra into my thinking, things seemed to be much easier to deal with.

Trust Your Instincts

When my daughter was very young (probably three or four years old), I remember playing a board game with her. As we were playing, she would have to make a decision about going in one direction or another. Sometimes she would pause and look at me with a questioning gaze and ask, "What do you think I should do Mama?"

I always answered the same way, "Trust your instincts, my pretty girl."

Now, I already told you she was inquisitive right? So of course, she asked, "What are instincts?"

I explained if she listened very carefully and felt a tingling feeling in her chest and tummy, those were her instincts and they were telling her what to do.

Do you really think we were done with the questions? Of course not! "How do I know they're telling me the right thing to do?" she asked.

I explained while she was still so little, she could think of her instincts as she would a Fairy Godmother who only wants the best for her and will help her get it. And as she got older, she would realize her instincts were a combination of intelligence and integrity that would guide her when making decisions.

Of course there were more questions, but the point of the matter is you need to be able to trust your instincts. Let me give you a word of caution here before you run off and do something crazy. You can only trust your instincts if the decisions you are making are founded on truth and love. If you are making decisions based on fear, anger, guilt, frustration, hate, or any other word opposite of truth and love, I guarantee you're making the wrong decision. This is not an area you can negotiate; you must make decisions out of truth and love.

Now, we all know we can't make decisions out of truth and love if we're living in a self-imposed world of fear, guilt, anger, or hatred; but let's face it, with all that is going on in your life right now, what are you supposed to do about getting rid of fear, guilt, anger, and hatred? Hmm, how about heal yourself; how about identify what is important, and how about letting it go.

Don't whine, I know these things aren't easy. You do recall I lived through this as well, but you can do it. Let's look at each of these things briefly.

Fear – Because of a devastating early life experience, I lived in fear for most of my life, and it's a terrible place to live.

I am convinced God gave me my daughter to help me come out of this world of fear, get the counseling I needed, and to live my life fearlessly. I thank Him for her and for the incentive to get help because it changed my life.

Guilt – As I mentioned earlier, I was raised Italian Catholic. I used to tell people my blood type was not O, or A, but rather ICG (Italian Catholic Guilt). Now, I know there are many ethnic and religious groups who believe they have the corner on guilt, but I don't think anyone would argue that Italian Catholics aren't way up on the list.

What is guilt? It's someone trying to get you to do or say something through manipulation; it's that simple. So when you make decisions based on guilt, they are directly contrary to the core of what decisions should be based on: truth and love. And by the way, if you had to be coerced to make the decision, then you weren't listening to your Fairy Godmother (Instinct) now were you?

When I turned 40, my birthday gift to myself was to give up guilt. I know that might sound strange (of course, you already think that about me) but it was one of the greatest gifts I gave myself. How do you do this? I had to first let go of what other people thought of me. I then gave up trash talking myself and followed up with a lot of extremely positive self-talk (see "Fake It Until You Make It"). Finally, I rewarded myself when I reacted to a decision without letting guilt influence me.

People, people, let me tell you, it was one of the most liberating things I've ever done, and I now have a life where guilt has no anchor. Another wonderful side benefit is if you don't receive guilt, you don't give it either. I think this is worth repeating. If you don't receive guilt, you don't give it either. How wonderful it would be for you and the people you interact with who are blessed with dealing with you on a more honest and non-manipulative level.

Anger – A strong feeling of displeasure and belligerence aroused by a wrong. It just seems to make sense if something was initiated with a "wrong," its outcome may be a "wrong" as well. If you make a decision when your mind is overwhelmed with a strong feeling of displeasure or belligerence, do you really think you're letting your intelligence guide you?

Anger interferes with our mental equilibrium and emotional distance, which makes it difficult for us to analyze the cause of our anger. This, in turn, makes it even harder to establish a constructive strategy for handling our anger.

Reacting from a place of anger can only hurt ourselves or others. So how do you avoid striking out (or within) because of anger? Find alternatives to angry behavior. Let's be clear on one concept here. I am not suggesting you don't get angry and I am not suggesting you stuff the anger. Hiding anger from yourself is not healthy and causes you more harm. The best thing is to find a way to work with angry emotions without causing harm.

For our fitness friends, taking a walk, jogging, lifting weights, or other forms of physical exercise may burn off some steam and help you get off the anger ledge and back on solid ground. For those not so fitness directed, blast the music, dance with an imaginary dance instructor who knows all the good moves, clean your house, write a vicious letter, scream into a pillow, better yet, punch the pillow (only after you imagine someone's face on it). You could also try gardening, making something from clay, or calling a venting buddy (one who listens, acknowledges, and then hangs up without judgment).

What you do NOT want to do is drink, drive a vehicle, operate equipment (even a sewing machine can be dangerous when you are distracted), lash out at the mail carrier (or some other innocent bystander), harbor your negativity, confront the offender, or any other action that could cause harm.

Try this: Write down a list of anger outlets *before* you need them and put them where you can easily find them. One time, I searched the house desperately for my list. Each room I combed without success frustrated me more. Finally, when I found the list, I tore it to shreds. (I was going to show it what would happen if it was not readily available.) Then, when my fit was over, no harm done, I carefully taped my list together. Now my wretched looking list is in the top drawer of my desk. Sometimes just looking at it in its sad shape makes me laugh and distracts me from my anger; giving me another safe outlet.

Hatred – Just looking at this word makes me cringe. I am no "rose-colored glasses" type of person (like my mother), but I just can't seem to wrap my head, heart, or spirit around hatred. From an intellectual point of view, I don't get it. From an emotional point of view, it feels like it can only be harmful to me. From my spirit's point of view, I just want to cry. Sorry I digressed so much, but the point is don't make decisions from a position of hatred.

A Better You

In the midst of a divorce, you might think you wouldn't have the time or energy to commit to a "better" you. But with a strong parenting plan, effective co-parenting communication skills, and a happy child, you can find the time, and you deserve it.

One resource which helped me during this reconstructive period was a book entitled *The Four Agreements* written by Don Miguel Ruiz. This book is worth delving into, and I loved the simplicity of the four agreements, which were:

1. Be Impeccable with Your Word,
2. Don't Take Anything Personally,
3. Don't Make Assumptions, and
4. Always Do Your Best.

If you're like me, when I first read the list, I said, "I betcha that's much easier said than done." After reading the book, I was right, but it was a great place to get started. I read the book when it first came out in 1997 and have been reading it every five years since then. I have made progress; however, I still have a long way to go. But I know I'm moving forward and I know the book contributed to making my life more peaceful and making me feel more whole and worthy. As I am writing this, Mr. Ruiz has written *The Fifth Agreement,* and as a gift to myself, I have promised to take an entire day off as soon as the first draft of my book is completed and spend the day on his book. I can't wait!

In addition to the ideas you'll pick up from *The Four Agreements,* several other life lessons may help:

Learn from Your Mistakes – No one is perfect (although some like to act like they are); we all make mistakes. In fact, I think mistakes are great for several reasons. They provide me with the opportunity to learn something new. They challenge me to maintain my positive self-image in spite of the mistake. They allow me to share my experiences with others so they won't make the same mistakes. They force me to re-evaluate and look at things from a different perspective. Heck, the more I write about them, the more I like mistakes. Find their value!

Overall Health — You need to check in on your physical, mental, emotional, and spiritual health and create a plan to help you improve your overall wellbeing. For me, I started doing yoga, took dance lessons (because I'm passionate about dancing; not very good at it, but passionate), maintained a healthy diet, spent time with friends, and went to a counselor when needed. There is no set plan that works for everyone. Start with a critical self-inventory and then make a plan (see the "Create a Plan" section in this chapter) and enjoy your successes.

Fake It Until You Make It

This topic is one of my favorite mantras. Scientific research has proven that what we tell our subconscious mind, it believes without question. When our subconscious mind hears something, it acts on it accordingly. Because of this connection between your words and your subconscious mind, affirmations are a powerful tool to change how you feel emotionally, mentally, and even physically. Without getting involved in a long discussion about affirmations, basically what you do is speak out loud what you want your subconscious to hear. If you say, "I feel great today," your subconscious mind says, "Okay," and starts acting in ways to reinforce the fact that you feel good. You're more alert, you walk with a spring in your step, you greet the world with a smile, and you have a good day. If you say, "I feel like doo-doo today," your subconscious mind again says, "Okay," and starts acting in ways to reinforce the fact that you feel lousy. You are sluggish, drag your feet, have a frown on your face, and the day turns into a nightmare.

Remember, your subconscious mind does not have a filter to say, "I don't believe you." So you can say anything you want and it is going to say, "Okay." Be sure you speak affirmations in the present tense because your subconscious mind lives in the moment (what a great idea).

That's what fake it until you make it is all about. You keep saying whatever it is you want to achieve, and your subconscious mind will work with you to achieve it. Stop smoking ("I am a non-smoker, I hate the smell of smoke."). Weight reduction ("I only eat what my body needs; I do not eat anything more.") Being open minded to your former spouse ("I always keep an open mind and heart when I speak with him.")

When you first start saying affirmations, it is weird because you know you are saying something that may not be true at the moment. While your conscious mind might say, "That's not true," your subconscious mind says "Okay." In the beginning it sounds weird, almost as if you were lying, and it feels a bit weird because your conscious mind is struggling with it. But after your first successful attempt with affirmations, you will start this huge list of things you are going to work on next. Just make sure getting along with your former spouse is near the top of the list, okay?

Affirmations have been proven to work. No, they do not work overnight, but they do work. Typically, it takes about three weeks to change a behavior. Start today. Commit to the three weeks, and start faking it until you make it.

CHAPTER 8

WEIRD STORIES

Don't say I didn't warn you that there were going to be some weird stories in this book. Even as I am writing them, I think they're weird, and I lived them. I guess the point of this section of the book is to let you know that when it comes to co-parenting your child, you'll end up doing things you never thought you would. The important thing here is to keep child-focused; it doesn't matter what other people think about you (if you truly believe it does matter, there is a whole slew of self-help books with your name on them). What matters is you're putting your money where your mouth is, you're walking the talk and you're stepping up to the plate (I'm sure there are a ton of other cliché-type quotes which can apply here). But you're doing what you need to do to provide your child with a stable family environment, even though the definition of family may be a bit different.

Second Grade

When our daughter was in second grade in public school, there was a countywide initiative (someone must have gotten a grant to do something), and all second grade students were interviewed by a psychologist to discuss family dynamics. The school notified us of the program (of course with the standard ability to opt out if we so desired) and then I completely forgot about the entire project until. Several weeks later, I got a voice mail from the principal. Since I volunteered at the school and was in there at least twice a week, I had a very good relationship with the principal and knew how much she loved our daughter. (But then again, who couldn't love her?)

When I returned her call, addressing her on a first name basis, I was shocked when she stated, in a very professional tone that she needed me to come to the school to speak with her and the psychologist. Of course I thought they were going to tell me how brilliant and well adjusted our daughter was so I went into the meeting with an open mind and optimistic attitude. When the psychologist asked if we had previous experiences where our daughter was known not to tell the truth, I was flabbergasted. One of the cardinal rules of our family is to tell the truth. (Refer back to the "About Truth" section in the "It's All About Me" chapter.) So I calmly explained that, to my knowledge, my daughter didn't even know what a white lie was, let alone any other type of lie. I further stated she has never said or behaved in a manner which led us to believe she was being devious, deceitful, or lying.

Note to daughter: In fact, you were so ridiculously forthcoming; there were times I was tempted to tell you that you didn't have to provide me with every single detail of your life. However, I am grateful we set the foundation early because we've been able to share a close connection that has served us both well. I was a bit more prepared for your teen years when you openly told me about various enlightening (yes, I mean frightening) experiences and you always had a person you could speak with to help you work through some difficult things. I love win-win!

Back to Second Grade

You know how people look at you when they think you are clueless; it's like when Southern people say, "Bless your heart," when actually they are saying, "You clueless idiot." Well that was the look on the psychologist's face when she proceeded to tell me my daughter told her the following:

1. Her father came to visit her every month,
2. I would pick him up at the airport,
3. He would stay at our house in the spare room,
4. We would always have at least one meal together over the weekend as a family (Rick would cook of course),
5. I would lend him my car so they could get around during the weekend, and

6. Sometimes the Parental Unit would all join in to put her to bed (and then share a glass of wine together – but she might not have known that tidbit).

As the psychologist was speaking, her tone of voice became more animated and she consistently looked at me to gain my reaction. Well, she might have been telling me something as interesting as my grocery list (you know how I hate domestic stuff) because I sat there straight faced until she stopped speaking. When she indicated our daughter had such a "vivid imagination" (aka, little liar), I confirmed everything she had said was, in fact, the truth. I also mentioned the holidays and birthday parties as well. I went so far as to suggest we set up an appointment with her the next time her father was in town so we could all discuss it.

The psychologist was so amazed that divorced parents could behave in such a manner; she asked if Rick and I would be willing to speak to other parents. I told her that Rick lived six hours away so I didn't think her idea was feasible (that's my story and I'm sticking to it).

Why Are You Not Married?

Rick and I did a great job of co-parenting and being civil to each other. Maybe too good a job, because when our daughter was about seven years old, she asked us why we weren't married. She and I had been living with Boukie for about four to five years, and she saw how happy we were together. However, the confusion for her came during Rick's monthly visits. When he arrived, we would give each other a hug and sit and talk for a little while. Thinking we were exposing our daughter to a loving environment, we never thought about any mixed messages to her, until well, "out of the mouths of babes…"

Rick and I discussed this and agreed from that point on to skip the hugs when he visited. After we talked we sat with her and explained that people could, and should, still care about each other even if they were no longer married. We also told her people who both loved the same person, just like how her father and I both loved her, worked together and were nice to each other so we could focus our attention on loving her. After this grand explanation, she asked, "Is it easy to be nice to each other?" Without skipping a beat, Rick and I looked at each other, laughed, and simultaneously said, "Not always."

And you know what? It is not always easy to be nice to people, especially a former spouse. However, each time you encounter that person, you have a choice, and within the choice, you have the power to choose what type of person you want to be in the moment. You can choose how you are going to behave and how you will receive what the other person is saying. Once you realize you have the power, you will also recognize the consequences of your actions are all yours. Choose wisely!

Florida to Disney

When we were preparing our parenting plan, Rick and I included a statement indicating that the first time our daughter would go to Disney would be with both of us. If either of us had remarried, the other spouse was invited to join us, but we did say the two of us would have to be there.

So when she was about five or six years old, Rick, our daughter, and I got in the car and drove to Disney. We spent about four days there and had a good time. Now you might think that was weird enough, but it isn't even the weird part of the story.

The weird part is while in Florida, we stayed with Rick's future in-laws. Yes, Rick had been dating a woman for some time, and I believe discussions were underway regarding their upcoming marriage. Since her parents lived right outside of Disney, I guess she and Rick discussed the idea of us staying there to save some money. Then they discussed it with her parents (who by the way, had NO reservations about taking us in). I have to admit I was a bit hesitant about this arrangement; I had never met these people, and it was my former husband's girlfriend's parents. How strange was that?

We pulled up into their driveway after being in the car far too long. It was almost midnight, and we were tired, cranky, and I was also very anxious. Well, you would have thought they were expecting some famous dignitaries because all of the house lights went on, the door flew open, and this diminutive woman and large burly man stood on the front stoop with arms thrown open wide.

After loving on our daughter and finally getting her to bed, the four adults sat outside by the pool and talked for hours. I felt welcomed and totally comfortable. But wait… it gets weirder still. Rick and I had to share a bedroom (how long should I pause here just to keep you guessing?) Fortunately, the room had two spare beds, but the most hysterical part is before we went to sleep, Rick's future mother-in-law stuck her head in the door and said, "Now don't do anything I wouldn't do. Oh wait, you've already done that. Well, just don't do it again."

We all went to bed laughing!

Rick's Wedding

We were living six hours away from Rick when he was getting married to the woman whose parents let us stay in their home when we went to Disney. Since our daughter was in the wedding, I agreed to drive her over, and I intended to stay in a hotel for the three days of the celebration. In fact, I actually intended to go to a spa as a treat for my "above and beyond" behavior.

We had a terrific ride over, and it was made more fun because we were traveling during the Christmas holiday season. There were cars from all over the country going to the several "destination" areas in that part of the country. Our daughter was writing down the states of the various license plates we saw. As I said it was a six-hour drive, did I mention that I hate driving? I think the longest anyone should drive is two hours and any distance longer should be reached by train, plane, or better yet, have the people come see you instead.

By the time we were about five hours into the trip, we had over 40 states identified, and we were very excited. I was approaching a car with a license plate I hadn't seen before. My daughter encouraged me to get close so we could see the plate clearly. No, I didn't get into a car accident; after all, I had precious cargo on board. But what I did do was miss the exit to get to Rick's and ended up having to drive an additional hour.

When we arrived, Rick was relieved to see us arrive safely, albeit just before our daughter was to go out to dinner with his in-laws and him. I said, "I'll just quickly help her get ready, and then I'll head to the hotel." He looked at me stunned and said, "I thought you were staying here, we have the guest bed made up in the living room." I thought the bride wouldn't want to wake up on her wedding day to see her soon-to-be-husband's former wife in the next room, but that was just me. But the bride did genuinely encourage me to stay. So I spent the evening in their home while they were rehearsing.

The next morning I actually helped the bride with her hair, and then, when they left for the church, I left for the spa. Who had the better end of that deal?

Holiday Pictures

When my daughter was three and moved away from family and friends, I started sending annual letters (ok, so I put them inside the Christmas card to take care of two objectives with one effort, but you already know how efficient I am). These letters would describe the events of our daughter's previous year, and I would get several copies of pictures of her throughout the year and include them with the letter.

Since I kept a calendar of the things we did during the year, I would just take the calendar out and start typing my letter without any thought of censoring it in any way. Then, I added pictures corresponding to the events I mentioned in the letter and off it went. I was unprepared for the number of letters and phone calls I got back from family and friends asking me if I was out of my mind. Well, I always thought I was a bit loony, but I didn't know what they were referring to.

With a variety of tones, from judgmental to incredulous, people were amazed how much Rick was a part of our daughter's life. Her birthday party, some school events, several holidays, and many family excursions (including our daughter and the entire Parental Unit) were captured in photos. Most people couldn't understand why we chose to make the sacrifices (emotional as well as financial) to provide such an environment for our child.

I calmly listened to their ranting and raving, and then simply said, "We did it because it was our choice. Our choice gave our daughter a stable and loving environment. Isn't that what all parents want?"

Spit on the Floor

This weird story is more of a parenting tip, but it is weird enough to belong here. When our daughter was very young, about three years old, Boukie and I were trying to get her to explore different foods. So we told her to try a bite of something new; if she didn't like it, she could spit it out and she wouldn't get in trouble. We also said she could have a spoonful of ice cream to get the bad taste out of her mouth. The first time, it happened, I think it was with an oyster. She tasted it, made a face, spit it out right on the floor, and ran to the freezer to get the ice cream. After the disaster was over, I said, "Ok, honey, go get the rubber gloves, get some paper towels, and clean up the food you spit out."

She protested, "I thought you said I wouldn't get into trouble."

I said, "You're not in trouble, but you can't expect other people to clean up after you."

She thought about it for a while and must have thought it made sense because she went to get the gloves.

I did suggest the next time this happened, she might consider spitting the food into a paper towel to avoid the clean up.

Rick was visiting one weekend and we ordered pizza. The entire Parental Unit likes anchovies on their pizza, so we got half the pizza with anchovies. Our daughter saw all of us eating "those hairy worms" but thought it was worth a try. She didn't like them and was desperately trying to find a paper towel and ended up reaching for Rick's t-shirt into which she spit the food. Boukie and I were laughing hysterically because Rick's face was worth a thousand words. When we explained what our thinking was behind trying new foods, he merely asked if he could use the washing machine.

Temper Tantrums

Here is another parenting tip that falls into the weird stories category. My daughter and I were in the library and she was excited about getting a book about hedgehogs. Well, the book wasn't available and she was very upset. It looked like she was about to start a temper tantrum, so I sat down on the floor in the library, grimaced my face, shook my arms in the air, and opened my mouth wide.

She sat next to me and asked, "What are you doing, Mama?"

I told her I was having a temper tantrum, but since it was the library, I had to do it quietly.

She said, "You're embarrassing me."

And I said, "Well, this is what a temper tantrum looks like and if you don't want me to have one in front of you, I would appreciate it if you didn't have one in front of me."

Hand to my heart, pinky promise, this is the truth; she never did.

Teaching a Budget

Here is another parenting tip you might think is weird as well. Whenever I took my daughter into the grocery store or a budget store, I would tell her to get her own cart and pick out some things she thought she might like to have. She had to stay next to me, she wasn't allowed to reach for items out of her reach, and she had to behave in the store. I told her, "If we have any money left over from our budget, we can look at buying you one of the items you have in your cart."

I always made sure I had about two dollars left over. After I completed my shopping, we would look at the money in my hand and determine how much we had. Then, we would look at the items she had selected and determine how many we could get. Finally, came the decision making process, which frankly would go on for about 10 minutes and she would then be responsible for taking her item and the money to the checkout person.

She always felt very good about her purchases and she always treated her possessions very well because I think she knew if she took care of things, they would last longer.

Everyday Living

As of this writing, my daughter is 21-years old and I just asked her if she could recall any other "weird" stories about her life.

She looked at me quizzically and said, "We had weird stories?" So I read her what I had written and she said, "What is so weird about those stories?"

My response was, "Well maybe weird is not the right word, but they are atypical."

She said, "All I know Mom, is that you guys love me, you gave me guidance, helped me learn new things, encouraged me to explore, and I always knew I could count on you, and I still can."

Who could ask for more?

A PARENTING PLAN

Since I started writing this book, I've found several states now have legislation requiring people to put together a parenting plan if they have children under the age of 12 when they are going through a divorce. I think this is a wonderful idea; back in 1994 when we did it, people just thought we were crazy.

Because of these laws, as well as increased awareness of what divorce can do to a child, you now have several resources to help you create a parenting plan. I just did an Internet search for parenting plan and got about 214,000,000 results in 0.31 seconds; so start there.

Since your plan needs to be unique to your own situation, I won't go into the details about our actual plan. You know how much I like to plan, but you have to do the work yourselves and it will be worth the effort, believe me. I'll give you some more insider tips.

Save Time and Money

People spend a great deal of time and energy creating a pre-nuptial agreement. Why? They want to protect their assets. It makes the same sense to create a post-nuptial agreement to avoid having to spend assets unnecessarily. Let's look at a potential scenario.

> You have a standard formal divorce which lays out all of the rules and regulations. Something minor happens, you call your lawyer, you take your spouse to court, the judge rules (for or against—doesn't matter at this point). Then, something else happens, and you repeat the pattern. After just a few repeat performances, you have spent considerable money on the attorney. In addition, the judge is sick of listening to your whining, you have consistently interrupted your life, and your former spouse is ready to completely abandon the divorce agreement because he feels he's never going to do anything right anyway, so why bother.
>
> You just turned sweating the small stuff into an art form that has cost you time, money, energy, and a spirit of cooperation. Now, something huge comes up, your spouse wants sole custody. By now, the lawyer only wants to see your open checkbook, not you. The judge doesn't want to see you at all, and may actually

think your spouse should have sole custody, and there you stand looking like the little boy who cried wolf.

Plan B

When it comes to your parenting plan, your plan B is just as important as any other aspect of the plan. You have thought about every school event, sporting event, holiday, vacation, medical and dental care, and other events that could occur in your child's life and have made a plan. But have you made a plan B for each of those situations? Things get chaotic when you are least prepared to handle them. This is exactly the time when you need a plan B. This way you can adjust quickly, without emotional turmoil, and achieve a desired outcome.

In every relationship, it seems one parent is more of a planner than the other (guess who?). So when you're creating a parenting plan, one is usually coming up with a huge list of things to plan for. The other person is rolling his or her eyes and begging for these discussions to end. This is normal. No one is doing anything wrong. But what ends up happening is the planner is pushing and shoving the process along, and the other person feels like they are being dragged, kicking and screaming, to the first day of kindergarten. Be sensitive to this difference. Plan accordingly. Set up several mini-meetings to deal with your parenting plan and run it like a meeting. Send out an invitation, prepare an agenda, make the atmosphere conducive to a productive exchange, and end the meeting with a discussion of the next steps (which may very well be another meeting.

Rome wasn't built in a day (I know, who cares?), but the point is take the time you need to do the job well. The stronger your plans, the more successful your co-parenting roles will be.

I remember one of our plan B items was to "drop back 10 and punt." At the time, I thought we were just trying to be funny, and lighten up the planning process. But over the years, I realized we have used this particular plan B quite often. To me it means, stop, take some time to think about what you're going to do, pray, and then endorse an action you both agree on (sort of). And during those rare moments when we don't agree (I know you think I am being facetious here, but truly we were able to agree 90% of the time – thanks to our plans and plan B), we would look at each other, grab the football, run outside, drop back 10 and punt.

MESSAGES FOR
KIDS OF DIVORCE

Here are some messages to provide support to kids involved in a divorce:

1. Divorce is sad; it's okay to feel sad. Talk about it and don't hold your emotions in.
2. While many families go through a divorce, it doesn't make it easier to deal with.
3. Just because your parents are going through a divorce doesn't mean your parents are uncaring people.
4. Your parents love you even if they're divorced.
5. You are not to blame, in any way, for your parents getting a divorce.

6. If you want to blame one parent for the divorce, you really need to blame both of them because divorce is not one person's fault.

7. People often get married because they want to live together, but those feelings don't always stay forever.

8. The definition of a family doesn't require everyone to live together.

9. Two people can try very hard to stay happily married but still end up divorced.

10. Just as it's hard to live apart from someone you love, it's just as hard to live with someone you don't love.

11. Everyone changes in different ways, and it is usually these changes that cause couples to go in different directions.

12. Even though it may not feel this way sometimes, both of your parents want to be happy, and they want you to be happy as well.

13. The reason you live with one parent more than the other does not mean one parent loves you more than the other.

14. It's okay to spend time with each parent alone. You can do cool things together and enjoy each other.

15. Your relationship with your parents is very special and doesn't have to change because of a divorce.

16. You may never completely understand why your parents divorced, but you should feel you can always talk to them about it.

Most importantly, if you find your child is struggling, get help. If your child is a bit more isolated, not eating sufficiently or eating more unhealthy foods, having school grades drop, being more secretive, pursue this sooner than later. You know your child better than anyone else. So you have to be vigilant about observing any modifications in their behaviors. Don't make excuses for these behaviors, such as "Well, he probably had a bad day," or, "Well, she is a teenager." Use some of the hints I provided in the "Life After Divorce" chapter to keep the communication channels wide open with your child.

Don't be vain about seeking help. Do NOT let finances (there are several inexpensive if not free options if you look for them) or insecurities interfere with you getting your child the help he or she needs. In fact, consider getting some help for yourself.

APPENDIX C

HELPFUL HINTS

These are just more insights from the journey I experienced. Some will be helpful and some may not be. Hopefully you'll understand this guide is a resource to help you succeed in being a successful co-parent and to make sure none of your words or actions are at your child's expense.

A

Alternatives to anger – Find non-destructive ways to deal with anger. Don't stuff anger because it'll always come back; instead, find ways to deal with it and get rid of it.

Adjust – Think Gumby (remember the green cartoon contortionist character); that is you from now on. You can do it.

Agree – On what is best for your child. Either agree harmoniously or agree to disagree, but agree nonetheless so your child is not put into the middle of a disagreement.

B

Be compassionate – It's amazing we can more easily be compassionate to a stranger than we can to someone we used to be married to. You're leaving the grocery store, and a man is putting up a poster about a lost dog. You stop, speak to him briefly about the loss, you might even touch his arm to show him you care, and you offer to keep your eyes open and to spread the word about his lost dog. Then you get home, get a phone call from your former spouse who states a problem he's having and you shut down. Thoughts of "Here we go again. What's his excuse now?" and "I'm sick of this," all go running through your head before he has spoken a word past "hello".

So how did I handle it? Easy, I imagined he was a stranger. I know this sounds silly, but it really worked. Whenever he called, I closed my eyes, imagined the man with the lost dog, and then opened my ears, mind, and heart to hear what my former husband had to say.

From that perspective, I can show compassion and even assist in resolving the problem. Boy has this made my life better. And by the way, the man did find his dog, and I bless the day I met him because he has been the one to help me find my way towards compassion.

Be proud of you and your efforts – There are going to be a lot of "firsts" as you transition from married to not married and there are going to be a lot of "lasts." Some of these situations will be easy for you to handle; others will not. The point here is to be proud of yourself. Instead of feeling overwhelmed or incompetent when your first home repair arises, head to the home improvement store. Ask questions of the people there who can guide you in fixing the problem. And you know what; it doesn't have to be perfect.

Breathe – Every time I say that word to people, they laugh at me. I teach yoga and water aerobics classes, and I am always reminding the class, "Breathing is not optional." They laugh until they get so focused on an isometric exercise that they forget to breathe. Breathe when you are frustrated; deep breaths will bring your blood pressure down. Breathe when you are worried; deep breaths are the number one cure for headaches. Breathe in appreciation, joy, and peace; breathe out anger, negativity, and grief. Just breathe.

C

Commit to success – There's a great deal of research on our body cells and how your cells can talk to you and you can talk to your cells. Research proves if you say something out loud your subconscious mind will unilaterally accept it and respond accordingly. Therefore, when you commit to success in your thought and language, your subconscious goes along for the ride. As a result, you're committing every cell of your being to success, and your body becomes more relaxed and more confident. Your emotional state is calmer, your focus is clear, and your heart is open to the other person and the process you are undertaking. You couldn't ask for a better state of being when discussing your parenting plan or resolving an issue about your child.

Create laughter – I don't think a day is complete without laughter. My mother always said, "Start each day striving to learn something new, end each day with prayer, and in between, laugh as much as you can." Bless her for giving me a blueprint for life and for being such a wonderful example. The one thing about my mother's laugh is that it was robust to say the least (and according to my daughter, I inherited this trait). I mean how much sound can one person make? If you were on one side of the mall and my mother starting laughing on the other side, I swear you could hear her. Of course during my teenage years, I was mortified whenever she laughed, and I think I did everything in my power to discourage her laughter (like most teens do). But now that she is gone, I seek daily to make sure I can hear her laughter in my internal ear and in my heart.

Count your blessings – Really count them. Make a list, look at the list, and appreciate what you have as well as what you don't have. To appreciate means to acknowledge what you have, to be aware of those blessings and to be grateful for them daily. Remember you DO have a choice about either appreciating where you are right now or to grumble and moan about these temporary changes. My list of blessings is so long it overshadows the life changes I've had to make now that I am a single mom, sole provider of the household and have no family nearby. So when the blues start tapping you on the shoulder, pull out your list and have a good long look it. You might find you can even add a thing or two to the list and lift your spirits too as you see how much you already have.

D

Differences – My mantra when it comes to differences is, "Difference is not necessarily right or wrong, it just is." What this statement allows us to do is look at the "difference" with a clear, unbiased perspective, and make decisions based on fact versus blinding emotionalism. When my daughter talks about the rules in her father's house being different from the rules in my house, we start by admitting that just because the rules are different doesn't make them right or wrong. By clearing the stage we can talk about these differences. I can help her come to a decision about which of these rules seem right for her and help her develop strategies to deal with the differences that don't seem right to her.

Difference, whether it's cultural, religious, or ethnic, is a significant part of our lives. The better able we are to equip our children with understanding, accepting, and handling differences, the happier and more productive their lives will be. Acceptance of difference eradicates bigotry and prejudice and allows our children, with open minds and hearts, to embrace all that is available to them. The wonderful side effect of working with our children on the topic of differences is it clears our minds and hearts as well.

Derogatory comments – When Rick and I got divorced, I made the commitment not to say anything derogatory about him to my daughter. Did I like it always? Well what do you think? But remember, I don't have to like it. It was a commitment I made to honor my daughter. Okay, so I got a little carried away with it and made sure every time my daughter asked about her father I had something nice to say about him. "Your father is very creative when it comes to making things, why don't you discuss your science project with him?" "Your father has a green thumb; you can ask him what his thoughts are about those plants." "Rick is a terrific cook; do you want to save this new recipe to make with him the next time he visits?" Even though I had to avoid rolling my eyes or the gag reflex, I do believe it was better than saying out loud some of the thoughts running through my head.

Don't sweat the small stuff – I know you're expecting me now to say, "And it's all small stuff," but I'm not going to (although that's a great book you might want to read). Let's face it, when we're in the middle of the proverbial STUFF hitting the fan, we don't think its small stuff. What I want you to do is not sweat the small stuff, so you can save your energy for the bigger things. I guess what I'm saying is: pick your battles. If we take on every little incident with a vengeance, we end up burnt out when we really need our stamina. If you don't use up your energy on the small stuff, it'll be there if you ever need it, and if you don't ever need it, you are blessed and more power to you.

E

Embrace change – What freaks people out about change is its usually unexpected, so you're caught off guard. When you plan for change, it doesn't seem so bad. Even if the outcome isn't exactly what you wanted, it doesn't seem quite as bad because you prepared yourself for change. You can't always prepare for change, but if you keep your eyes, ears, heart, and mind open to be more aware of what is happening in your life, you may be a bit more prepared. Another aspect of change, which causes people to resist it, is their first reaction. "Oh no, what now?" seems to be the first thought when change arises. With that kind of negativity, your body and mind immediately go into defense mode, and you dig your heels into the ground and vow not to move from your current spot. If your reaction to change is, "Oh what an adventure this could be," can you imagine the fun and joy you would experience as you deal with the change? So I guess I am saying, change your perspective. Be prepared, change your perspective, and embrace change.

Empower your child – During a time of stress or change, as parents, we want to protect our children. This is a normal parental instinct, and it's an appropriate behavior. But it's during this time of protection that we, without realizing it, take power away from our children. It helps to give your child practice in making decisions. You've already given them a safe place to talk (refer back to "Giving Them a Place to Vent"); now you have to guide them in making decisions and plans. A good place to start is to ask questions to help them decide a course of action to take so they feel they did everything they could to prepare. Regrettably, at times, the plan may not go as intended, but you have to let your child experience the natural consequences and learn from these little mistakes. This is so difficult to do because we never want to see our children suffer, but these little learning experiences actually make them feel more empowered. So don't blow the game in the bottom of the ninth – bite your tongue, sit on your hands, and be there with open arms and soothing words.

Enemies—who needs them? – A natural response for many people going through a divorce is to make the other parent an enemy. They hurt you or they don't parent like you do or they took all of your mutual friends with them or whatever. No matter what your justification is for making the other parent an enemy, you have to ask yourself, "Who needs enemies?" Now, I'm not suggesting you become BFFs for life, but other than abuse, what reason do you have to make your former spouse an enemy? Let's face it. Do you really want to spend the rest of your child's life fighting the enemy over every little thing that arises? That makes me exhausted just writing about it.

F

Find sounding board(s) – A sounding board is a place or person where you can go, say anything you want, in whatever tone you want, and know you're not going to hurt or be judged by the other person.

Okay folks, let me help you wake up and smell the coffee, there is no such place. As wonderful as my best friend is, how truly open–minded, loving, non–judgmental, caring, and so on and so on, she's still a human being. While she may be very supportive time and time and time again, it starts to strain the relationship.

If you have been divorced for over three years, think about it. Who were the people you went to during your divorce? What is your relationship with them now? See, in some cases you don't even stay in touch with those people now, and even if you do, the relationship is not the same. Therefore, you need to share the misery among a group of friends (or even strangers; after all, look how nice you've been to them). The point is by sharing the pain, so to speak, your entire relationship with your once best friend does not get destroyed because of your divorce.

Friendly, not friends – I was telling a female friend of mine who is going through a divorce about the book I'm writing about child–friendly divorce.

She said, "I don't think I could ever be friends with my ex, I can barely stand to look at him."

I asked her if she recently went to the post office, grocery store, or some other store where she saw a person whose looks bothered her.

She said, "Yes, as a matter of fact, there's a guy at the grocery store who kind of gives me the creeps."

I said, "How do you treat him?"

She looked at me quizzically and said, "Well, I'm pleasant because otherwise it would be rude."

I said, "Well, imagine your ex is the guy from the store and treat him with the same courtesy."

She sort of chuckled and said, "Yeah, right."

I said, "I'm serious. I never asked you to be friends with your former husband, but I am strongly suggesting you treat him with the same basic consideration you give a stranger."

Forget about it – Now, I have really gone too far. Yes, I'm telling you to forget about things that prevent you from healing and moving forward. I know it's easier said than done. Here are some strategies which might help:

1. Ask yourself if in five years you will even remember this (if not, don't wait five years).

2. Ask if holding onto this thing is taking power away from you (take your power back by getting rid it).

If you think I am asking too much of you to "forget about it" let me assure you. If you don't let it go, you'll have to forgive. Which do you want to do?

Forgive – Let's remember I gave you the chance to "forgettaboutit," but there are some things you are still holding onto. So now you have to listen to my sermon on forgiveness (or skip ahead, but you know you'll come back and read this at some point). I struggled with forgiveness about an event which happened when I was a child. The event altered how I felt about myself and thus, changed the course of my life. I tried to forget about it, and I achieved some level of success. However, I only became completely free from the experience when…. Yes, you guessed right, when I forgave the person who caused me pain. With forgiveness, you can take back the power you inadvertently gave to another person or event, and you are free to heal.

G

Generate a plan before you need it – I'm not sure how much of my obsessive planning skills have come out in this book, but when I did a search for the word plan, my computer complained about the excessive volume. However, if you ask my daughter, she'll tell you that for just about every situation I not only have a plan but a Plan B and C as well. Here's my thinking, if you create a plan with several options, then when a situation arises, even if it is a stressful situation, you can make a decision based on your well-thought-out plan, not a reactive response to something that came up unexpectedly. Go ahead, call me silly, plans give me a sense of comfort and confidence. A lot of people would say I worry too much, that's the reason for all the planning. I say people worry too much because they don't have a plan. Once you have thought things out you can leave the worry behind.

Get off the seesaw – One day you're feeling on top of the world, making all of the right decisions and feeling good about you. The next day, some minor event occurs, and you plummet to the depths of self–doubt, self–deprecation, and a wholehearted fear you'll never again make a good decision. How do you get off the emotional seesaw? Take one step. That's right, just one step in a different direction. When you think about taking just one step, it doesn't seem to be a big deal. You can do it. But what's the point? What's one step going to do for me when I am feeling like I am being sucked into quicksand and will soon perish? Well, one step does several positive things. It makes you realize you have a choice, it moves you one step further away from the crisis, it distracts you from the pity party or revenge daydream you are having, and it might be just the step that starts putting you into a state of balance. From this state of balance, you can be clear, calm, and feel more confident about your decisions. Who knows, when you're feeling good, you might just take another step.

Get rid of negative influences – No, you cannot get rid of your former spouse, unless he is a negative influence and harmful to your child. I don't think I need to tell anyone what to do about that. However, when people are going through a tough time, the last thing they want to add to their plate is more troubling things. When we are horribly stressed out, some of us reach for a glass of wine and others don't get out of bed. When I'm stressed, I make sure there is no junk food in the house. You know what your vices are. Try to be sure these negative influences, whether they are gossipy friends, alcohol, or gallons of ice cream, are removed from your life when you are stressed.

H

Have meetings – The first time you have a meeting with your former spouse, you might decide to create an agenda so you have a frame of reference for those topics you need to discuss. The agenda helps keep you focused and prevents running off on a tangent. Several months after our divorce a friend of mine called and said, "I saw you with Rick at the local pub, and the two of you looked really cozy. Is there a chance of a reconciliation brewing here?"

If she had known we were struggling with a significant issue during the meeting, she might not have read into the situation further. Just goes to show you can't judge a book by its cover. Having a meeting in a public place, like a pub or coffee shop is a great idea because it sets some parameters to behave in a more civil manner. And the next time you don't want to have a meeting, keep in mind it's better to have a meeting with your former spouse than it is to have a root canal or annual physical exam, and you do both of those!

Honor your child – Many people say the most painful experience a person can go through is the birth process. Of course, all of those people have had children. So if you went through all of the trouble to have a child, the least you can do is to honor the result.

You often hear parents say, "I'd give my life for my child." So if you're willing to do whatever you have to do to protect and nurture your child, start with honoring her. What exactly does it mean? Well, I don't know for you, but I can tell you what it means for me. When her father left, I vowed I'd never say anything derogatory to her about her father. I know I've said this several times throughout this book; however if you do say nasty things about your ex to your child, it will always do more harm in the long run then keeping those comments to yourself. I'd answer her questions honestly. I'd give her a place to feel safe to discuss her feelings. I'd give her responsibility for those things she could handle. And I'd do what I could to nurture her relationship with her father and his family. Start there, that'll keep you busy for a while.

Honesty – Another part of honoring your child is answering her questions honestly. Here's a common scenario.

"How come you and daddy are not married anymore?"

"Because your father left the marriage when he chose to look for other things in his life."

"Do you still love daddy?"

"I love him for being a part of you and for helping raise you."

Don't even go to where I could have gone with those questions. There is no reason to, and it won't do anyone any good. The secret to success here is to not elaborate. Answer the question honestly. If your child is like mine and she has more questions, then she'll ask them, and you'll have to answer them. Just be succinct and honest.

I

If it works, keep doing it; if it's not working, stop – Again, simple words which are often difficult to implement. But for me, these words help me maintain consistency. Being consistent with your child provides a great deal of comfort. For my child, she often got frustrated because she KNEW what your answer was going to be and she also KNEW (her eyes rolling by now) the Parental Unit would agree. There is no way she could weasel another outcome. While the experience may have been frustrating and annoying to her, the consistency provided her with reassurance and security.

The second part of this hint is also difficult to implement; just ask a smoker. Research says it takes three weeks to develop a pattern or habit but at least three months to break it. So be patient. If you've been doing something that isn't working, stop and keep stopping for three months and free yourself from the habit.

If you can't stand the heat – The rest of the expression is "then get out of the kitchen." Love the concept; it's right up my ally. I've never been good in the kitchen anyway, so why would I stay there when I don't need to. But in this case, we're going to focus on what creates the heat and what actions we can take to get out of the kitchen without running away from the situation. As far as I'm concerned, the fire extinguishers you can use are patience, focus, and love.

If you keep your focus, maintain patience, and know your efforts are being expended out of the love you have for your child, you might be able to avoid the heat.

It's a process, not an event – My daughter has heard this statement a thousand times in her life. Often people have a desired outcome, and when they don't realize that outcome, they think the effort was not worth it. It's in these situations where, "enjoy the process" comes into play. Take writing this book, for example. I love sitting down each day, sharing my thoughts and ideas. Having gone through the process of getting a previous book published, I know the outcome is difficult to achieve. With the previous book, I received 203 rejection letters before the book was published. If I had been focused solely on the outcome and didn't enjoy the process, I wouldn't be sitting here right now.

J

Joy is in the moment – When we see a beautiful sunset, watch the first robin hopping around with a worm, view a breathtaking rainbow, or see the glee in a child's eye, we know what joy is all about. But what about the joy we can find in making pancakes in the morning, taking in clean clothes from the clothesline, successfully reconciling the checkbook, completing a job at work on time, and so on? See the pattern? I am taking each one of your daily life activities and telling you to find joy in them. I'm not the queen of domesticity (if you haven't gotten the memo yet), and I have to juggle work, parenting, household chores, volunteer activities, and so much more on a daily basis.

So finding joy in daily activities might suggest to you I must be taking some happy pills (not everything is about wine).

Alas, there are no pills, but there's a choice. Here I go again, talking about choices, but you know what, when all else fails, knowing I have a choice gives me peace of mind, comfort, and a sense of control. I can crab and moan about how I didn't get a good night's sleep. I can grieve about pancakes being just a little too lumpy and a little crispy around the edges. I can even curse the clothing gods for not making matching outfits for adults. OR, I can thank God for a new day, draw happy faces with syrup to cover up the burnt edges and lumps, and close my eyes, stick my hand in the closet, and wear whatever comes out. It's simply a matter of choice. But let's look at the results. If you start the day crabby, out of sorts, and frustrated, how do you think the day is going to turn out? Go ahead, take those imaginary happy pills, be goofy, laugh a lot, choose to be happy, and you'll find the joy in the moment.

Just do it – While the athletic footwear company made this tag line famous, it's something we can use in our daily life. In reality, there are some things you need to do, but you don't want to do. However, just do it. Eat the frog, take a step, make a choice, and just do it. I know how difficult it can be, so sometimes I will reward myself for doing something I don't want to do. The reward might be a nice long bath or a piece of chocolate (I really mean an entire bag of chocolate), or it might be finding time to have a long conversation with a friend. Whatever you can do to entice yourself to just do it, especially when you don't want to, go ahead, take the first step and just do it.

Jump off the dead horse – I've always told my daughter she should pursue things until they don't make sense. It was a concept I used professionally which resulted in me being very innovative and forward thinking in my business. It's also a concept that encourages me to be more open-minded and open-hearted to new situations and experiences. However, at some point, the thing you're pursuing may no longer make sense, and you need to learn to jump off the dead horse. Stop banging your head against the wall, and let it go. Sometimes it's very difficult to do, especially when you are emotionally invested, but in the long run, you do realize the dead horse will never take you to your destination.

K

Keep it simple – The acronym KISS translates into **K**eep **I**t **S**imple **S**tupid. Many people change the last word to "silly" or a more gentle word starting with the letter s, but I like keeping the word "stupid" in there because it helps me remember if I don't keep it simple, then I may end up behaving in a stupid manner. Since I got rid of negative self-talk almost 20 years ago, I would never refer to myself as stupid, but if I keep on doing things in a more complex manner which creates chaos, then the end result is stupid behavior.

Keep it simple in your communications with your child and with her father. Keep your daily routine as simple as possible and don't add more to your plate than you can handle. Keep your expectations simple. It is better to be pleasantly surprised than devastatingly disappointed (another expression my daughter could quote in her sleep).

Kick out evaluation and interference – It seems for every event in your life, people love to come out of the woodwork with advice, suggestions, helpful hints, opinions, etc. This is a tough one to reconcile because on the one hand, I am obviously making suggestions and providing helpful hints to you in this book, so I do believe seeking help from others can be a good idea. If those opinions are evaluative, judgmental, and are interfering with your commitment to heal yourself and move forward, then kick them out.

When my daughter was born I was 39 years old, I was feeling totally unprepared for this entire parenting experience. A friend of mine said, "Listen to what people have to say, but only hear what makes sense." I didn't really understand the statement at first, but the more I thought about it (and believe me I think about things so much I do make myself crazy sometimes), I realized the values of the sentence. "Listen to what people have to say" suggests to me to be open-minded and open-hearted to people's thoughts, which gave me a larger pool of information to work with. "Only hear what makes sense" helped me put these thoughts through a sieve and weed out the ones which didn't seem right with my thoughts, feelings, and intuition. It helped me to trust my gut more and provided me with a wealth of ideas to choose from.

Knock it off – Right now, stop. Stop for just a moment and think about the past five minutes. Were you thinking good things about yourself? Were you working within your plan? Were you finding joy in the moment? I'm sure I'm going to hear a resounding "yes" to each of those questions. If not, why not? What did you do in the last five minutes which may have caused you angst, emotional self-harm, or lack of productivity? Knock it off. Rethink, reframe, refocus and get back on track to your more healthy and enjoyable life choices.

L

Lemonade; make it – Finances were probably one of the biggest concerns I had in raising my daughter. We just never had any extra money to do some special things. Instead of bemoaning my limitations, I found ways to work around them. My then two-year old and I went out to dinner once a week. Well actually, we stayed at home, but we pretended we went out to dinner. We dressed up, lit candles, and I even acted out being a waitress, which she was quite amused with. I bought my favorite foods and "ordered" what I wanted to eat. With multiple baby food options, she got to do the same. (Warning, a two year olds way of returning food she didn't want meant it went flying on the floor).

Another night, I gave us both manicures. I never realized how tough it is to paint with your left hand when you are right handed, but hey after a few shots, it was passable. I used nail polish, and I gave her washable paints. We put on plastic ponchos, sat on the kitchen floor with newspaper spread out, and had a grand old time. Actually, I think she did a better job than I did, and we had fun.

So as you can see, my daughter and I took lemons and made lemonades. By the way, the tart taste of lemons combined with the sweetness of sugar used to make delicious lemonade made me think that is what life is all about, combining the tart with the sweet.

Lose the guilt – Many ethnic and religious groups feel they have the market on guilt. For many of us, myself included, it was a way of life growing up. Guilt is defined as "feeling responsible for an offense or wrongdoing." Based on this definition, I guess if you don't want to feel guilty, all you have to do is not take responsibility for an offense or wrongdoing. Better yet, avoid offenses and wrongdoings all together. Well, I can't advocate not taking responsibility; we would become reckless and careless. And if we totally avoided offenses and wrongdoings, we would not be human. Sounds like we are stuck. Well, we're not.

We ARE going to make mistakes. When we make a mistake, we can do one of a couple of things. We can acknowledge our mistake, ask for forgiveness, learn from it, and move on. OR, we can hold tightly to the mistake and the associated consequences, and let the tentacles of guilt tear us apart. Neither course of action is easy nor painless. Remember the all important word here, CHOICE. One course of action guarantees release, peace of mind, harmony, and growth. The other just about guarantees self-loathing, ulcers, negativity, and a cycle of dismay. You have the power to choose. You pick.

Live for today – Some people have a tendency to live in the past, especially during a divorce. They think about what was, what went wrong, and wonder when it went wrong, how it went wrong. By doing so, these people keep their attentions focused on their past married life. Other people live with their eyes focused on the future, planning for what is going to happen tomorrow, and how you can change the future to meet your needs.

If we are living in the past or in the future, what the heck are we doing about today? Living for today really is a difficult concept to understand. I think the reason we don't do it more is we don't understand how to do it. How can we not think about the past if we are supposed to learn from our prior experiences? How can we not plan for the future? If we don't, where are we going to get the money for our kid's college tuition? So it seems the concept of living for today really doesn't make sense. However, I think this suggestion is intended to remind us to stay present and find joy in the moment.

M

Make choices – You can't always choose what happens to you in life, but you always get to choose how you react to each and every situation. The ability to choose gives you all the power. I have a friend, who is a CPA, and each tax season she moans, "I'm working too many hours, eating too much junk food, gaining weight, not going to the gym, and I barely get any sleep." We discussed choices and she realized there were some of those situations she could actually change. She could bring healthy food and snacks to the office and walk the staircase instead of using the elevator (both activities would have a positive impact on the weight situation). I then suggested she change her attitude about her workload. I suggested she focus on the grateful clients she has who really appreciate everything she does for them. At the end of tax season, she looked fit and happy and said she never realized how powerful making a choice could be. Choose to have the power; choose to seek joy and peace. It's your choice.

Mix curiosity with caution – At times when we are feeling vulnerable, we have a tendency to withdraw into a small, safe world which makes us feel less scared. At times, that is a good place to go. In this place, you can allow yourself to relax and come to grips with your fear. However, you can't live in that tiny little circle for long. Life just doesn't allow it. So what you need to do is mix curiosity with caution. Take a peek outside the door, see what's out there. You don't have to go out and join the rest of the world just yet, but at least look out the door.

Don't let your cautious routines entrap you. Try something new. Before I had my daughter, I had a perception of myself as being loving and realistic. I have a very good head for business, am quite successful professionally, am relatively athletically inclined, am a good dancer, and a voracious reader. What I am not is domestic. Cleaning the house, preparing and cooking meals, and trying to figure out which shoes went with which outfit were skills I simply didn't have. When it came to activities, such as sewing, knitting, arts and crafts, I didn't even think about trying any of those. I felt no talent, no interest, not going to happen. I thought my perception of myself was based in reality and was balanced. I would use my talents well, enjoy myself and simply find "workarounds" for those areas in which I wasn't quite as talented. I hired a cleaning person, set up a monthly meal calendar (which I never changed), and begged my "shopaholic" friend to buy all my clothes and write up a list of what I was suppose to wear with what. No biggie, things worked out well.

But then, when my daughter was 18 months old, her father left, and things had to change. I had to start mixing curiosity with caution, not only because my lifestyle was changing, but also because my daughter, the little Queen of Crafts, forced me to throw away some restricting perceptions and try new things. While this example seems minor, the point is there are times you want to take a look at the cautious world you have created for yourself and start thinking with more curiosity. Did you ever think a person who constantly pricked her finger while threading a needle would ever be able to make her daughter's wedding dress? More importantly, I'm curious enough now just to see what will happen (any simple, elegant patterns are welcome).

Mix caution with curiosity – A quick note for those of you on the other end of the spectrum, those of you who throw caution to the wind and run headlong into who knows what. You know who you are. You run off, half-cocked, do something way outside the realm of your comfort level, and then live to regret it. It may be something as minor as completely changing your hair color to something as radical as seeing just how many affairs you can have in six months. At either end of the spectrum, you still want to take a minute to stop, think about what you are planning to do, and ask yourself if you are comfortable with the decision. Better yet ask yourself if you would be comfortable if your daughter made the same decision (ah a bit of caution at it's best) and then take action.

N

No hidden agendas – Whenever you have a meeting with your former spouse, one of the most important aspects is to NOT have any hidden agendas. When my best friend had her first meeting with her former spouse, he suggested they go to a cocktail lounge. As it turned out, it was his new "watering hole." During the course of their meeting, they were interrupted several times by greetings from his "new" friends (male and female alike). It was clear her former husband had a hidden agenda which included, "I'm doing fine without you; see I have new friends and am well liked." She had to force herself to keep on task, maintain a pleasant demeanor, and get through the meeting.

Fortunately for us, Rick and I could always speak rather openly to each other so we got to avoid the "hidden agenda" drama.

Nurture relationships – Encourage your child to take responsibility for maintaining relationships with your former in-laws while you support the process to nurture those relationships. Each year, my daughter and I put together a calendar of her father's relative's birthdays and anniversaries. She went to the store with me to buy cards, and she was responsible for decorating them or doing whatever she wanted (sometimes she made bookmarks or other objects) to personalize them. Then, I gave her the address list, and she addressed the envelopes. We also marked on her calendar who she called each week (she rotated calling her grandparents, uncles, aunts, etc.), so she kept in touch with her father's family on a regular basis. I gave her the responsibility (and help when she needed it), and I also nurtured the relationships (buying the materials and paying for the phone calls). I also asked her about the conversations she had with her relatives, and we discussed her thoughts and feelings.

Never give up – I'm sure you realize this journey of a constructive divorce and a civilized relationship with your former spouse for your child's sake is not a straight path. You'll have setbacks and you'll have successes. You'll be fueled by successes to continue your efforts, but you'll also be persuaded to "hang it up" when obstacles get in your way. Parenting is not a job for the weak-spirited or the undetermined. It's a job which requires strength, wisdom, patience, an inquiring mind, and an open heart. My daughter is not living at home anymore and I foolishly thought my parenting role would lighten up a bit by now. WRONG!

Yes, our roles as parents change; actually change is the only constant thing we have in our roles as parents. So change you will. Many times you'll feel unprepared or overwhelmed by the responsibilities associated with parenting. Here is when you call upon your personal network; whether it includes your spiritual faith, the wisdom of your elders, the support of family, the compassion of friends, a review of this book or some other book, or even a visit to a counselor. Whatever you need to do to help you in your role as a parent, in a healthy and constructive way, is where you need to turn for help.

O

Of course it's going to hurt – No one said having a constructive divorce would be easy, and many times, it's quite difficult. You'll feel anger, hurt, resentment, disappointment, and a whole range of other emotions. Guess what? That's life. No, I'm not being flippant (although it may sound as if I am), but really, life is tough. Life brings good things, bad things, and things that are going to hurt you. We can't turn away from hurtful things, or we would end up living in a bubble. We have to prepare for the hurt and come up with ways to help us heal. When I reread this book (which an author does incessantly), I realized quite a bit of the book is about healing, and I hope the suggestions I've provided will help you heal. Come up with your own list of things you can do when you're hurt. A pity party often feels good (but limit the time for your own sake). Going for a long walk on one of your favorite trails might be a better idea. Doing some aggressive aerobic activity (such as kicking your former's butt; oh, wait, did I say that out loud?) may help you work out some frustrations.

I hate to bring up planning yet again, but do take a few minutes to put some thoughts together about what you can do when you're hurt (because we all know it's going to happen). It'll be good to have a safe place you can go to when you need it.

Open heart, open mind – Keeping your heart and mind open will help you learn new things. The beautiful thing about this helpful hint is opening your heart and mind is completely within your control. Be brave enough to step outside your comfort zone and mindful of keeping your focus. What helped me choose to do difficult things were the ideas presented in the "Fake It Until You Make It" section.

Another helpful tool was a spirit of adventure. Now, it has become abundantly clear to each of you that I do not like domestic activities. So when my daughter decided she wanted a birthday party with a Harry Potter theme, I was at my wits end. But with a spirit of adventure, I created magic wands by taking empty paper towel tubes, pinching the ends, filling them with baking powder, covering the tops with aluminum foil and putting little holes in the tops. When the children waved the wands, magic fairy dust came out. What in the world made me think to make those wands? Well, they say necessity is the mother of invention (or something like that), but it was my spirit of adventure that opened my mind to the creation. By the way, feel free to use my creation (no patent is pending).

Other shoes; put yourself there – We have all heard the expression, "You don't know what it's like until you walk a mile in another person's shoes." This thought has been helpful for me when I have had difficulty dealing with some people. I've used this concept in my professional life as well as my personal life, and it has always provided me with something valuable. Sometimes, it helps me understand the frustrations or angst the other person may be having. Sometimes, it helps me view the person in a different light. Sometimes, it makes me laugh to see myself in their footwear.

The underlying message here is it's important to gather as much information about a person or a situation before you make a judgment or decision. After gathering as much information as possible, you don't have to change your original opinion, but at least you have made the effort to not jump to conclusions.

P

Pray – Throughout this book, I have purposely avoided mentioning my spiritual beliefs because my Mama always told me to avoid discussions on politics and religion. People have their own beliefs, and I'm certainly not here to tell you what to believe. However, for me personally, prayer is a constant in my life, my parenting journey, and especially during the times I encounter difficulty implementing this constructive divorce and co–parenting plan. Prayer helps me remember the things I'm grateful for every day. For this reason alone, prayer is a valuable part of my daily life. For me, prayer is simply a conversation and not a once or twice a day thing. Heck, some days, it seems the only valuable conversations I have are the ones I have in prayer.

Again, I'm not telling you to pray, to whom you should pray, or how you should pray. I guess I'm suggesting you consider prayer as part of the support network you want to expand as much as possible. Prayer has saved my sanity, provided me comfort, given me insights, talked me off the ledge, softened my heart, and helped me maintain balance in my life.

Practice Patience – We've all had those days where it seems that everything goes wrong from the minute you open your eyes. You realize that the alarm didn't go off and now you are late for getting yourself and your child ready for the day. Of course, your last pair of nylons has a huge run (down the center no less), and the milk that you intended to pour on her breakfast cereal has the distinct odor of being way out of date. You could run around like a raving lunatic, screaming at your child to hurry up, OR, you could practice patience.

The idea of stopping for a moment to re-evaluate the situation when you are already late seems ludicrous, but let's plays that out. Stop, take a deep breath and think things through. So today, you wear slacks instead of a skirt and breakfast is peanut butter toast instead of cereal. See, no biggie.

By taking that moment to practice patience, you can find a (yes, say it with me) a Plan B that may even turn out better than your original plan. At the very least, you will have a much more pleasant start to your day than you would have.

Poo – No, I am not talking about Winnie; this Poo was one of my daughter's "Aunnies." This is a woman I first worked with and then became friends. Her name is Paula; however, her name was a mouthful for my daughter, so she called her Aunnie Poo. As with all good Aunnies, my daughter enjoyed spending time with Aunnie Poo. Also, it was a tremendous break for me because I could leave my daughter with her and feel comfortable to go about doing whatever it was I needed to do. I don't know all of the fun things they did together, but I did receive a very valuable lesson from Aunnie Poo.

It wasn't until years later this lesson became apparent, but I thank her to this day for it. One day when my daughter was in her tweens and going through an emotional angst, I listened to her and then immediately went into "fix it" mode. I came up with a list of things she might want to try to fix this situation. None of my ideas seemed to make my daughter feel any better. Finally, she got up and said, "Can I just sit in your lap and you hug me and let me cry?"

I said, "Well, of course."

So we did and she felt better.

Afterwards, she said to me, "Whenever I talked to Aunnie Poo about something I was sad about, the first thing she would say is 'Do you want me to just hear you or do you want me to help you fix it,' and it always made me feel better knowing that it was okay for me just to feel bad for a while."

From that point on, whenever my daughter had some emotional issue, she could say, "Mama, I need you to be Aunnie Poo." And I would know what she wanted from me. Thanks Aunnie.

Q

Quit whining and start winning – It's about attitude. There are tons of self-help articles about attitude and how it influences your thoughts, emotions, and behaviors. Your attitude affects how you feel about yourself and how you interact with others both personally and professionally. You have probably read articles about "reframing" your thinking. This concept deals with how you perceive a situation and how you can actively choose to alter the perception.

Let's take a simple example. You're trying to get through your grocery shopping, but several of the items you want to purchase are not in stock. You could whine about it, get frustrated, yell at a store manager, and leave without your groceries, or you could reframe the situation and look for an alternate product you haven't tried before. You check out a few other similar products and find one with the same ingredients and has the benefit of costing less. Still hesitant, you take the product home, try it, and learn you like it as much, if not better, than the one you previously bought. You choose.

Quiet time – Taking time for yourself may seem like a dream on some days, but it's important to carve out a few minutes of "me" time each day to reflect and rejuvenate. Some people I know do not leave their bedroom in the morning until they spend about 10 minutes stretching; others take the 10 minutes in prayer. While others take the extra time in a hot shower, it doesn't really matter what activity you perform. What matters is you focus on you and take the time to reflect and rejuvenate.

With the benefits of being open-minded, openhearted, and feeling good about yourself, you can get your day started in a much better light. Some people find it's a good habit to spend quiet time at the end of the day; sipping a warm glass of milk, reading something motivational, or enjoying a warm bath. In fact, science supports these suggestions. Such a small investment of your time can have an enormous return for you and those you deal with.

Quench your needs – Take care of you. If you don't, who will? It's often difficult, especially for parents, to focus on themselves. If you become physically worn out, emotionally drained, and spiritually depleted, there isn't much you can do for yourself or others. It makes sense to take care of yourself, but many of us don't do it. Why not? For me, it took a long time to differentiate between selfish and self-care. I felt whenever my focus was on my needs, I was being selfish, and I avoided responding to my needs.

My sister-in-law came to visit me shortly after my daughter was born, and when she saw me, she proclaimed, "You look like death warmed over. You're going to bed and you will only get out of bed to use the bathroom. You will do what I tell you for as long as I tell you until you return to the land of the living."

During the three days I stayed in bed, I slept. When she brought my meals to me, she would visit and chat. Then I would go back to sleep. While it felt like a dream to have this respite, I also felt she was "spoiling" me. We talked about my mixed emotions about her care and she said, "You were on the verge of collapse, and it never crossed your mind to meet your own needs."

She helped me understand the difference between selfish and self-care and even suggested I take time EVERY day to quench my needs. After three days in bed, my sister-in-law stayed for another week and helped me make this transition. Twenty years later, I still thank her for her honesty (although I think "death warmed over" was a bit harsh), I thank her for her guidance, and I thank her for giving me the opportunity to practice this new skill under her tutelage. I am definitely going to pay it forward to someone in need; it was a great gift!

R

Really, really? – Throughout the years, my friends and acquaintances have often been alarmed when they come to my home and Rick is there. "What is *he* doing here?" "Are you out of your mind?" "Doesn't it creep you out to wake up and see him come out of the other room?"

These frequently asked questions have always made me laugh. "He's here because we have to do something with our daughter." "He's here visiting his daughter." "No, I don't think I am out of my mind because I am supporting my daughter's relationship with her father." "Yes, it is a bit creepy, but it's a small price to pay for the benefits my daughter receives."

So when my best friend says, "Really, J, really?" I laugh with her and say, "Yes, Con, really."

Rinse and repeat – Many hair and facial products provide instruction for their use and end with "rinse and repeat." I always wondered about rinse and repeat. I used to think these companies just wanted me to use more of the product than I really needed to so I would have to buy the product more often (which may very well be the case). However, for me, rinse and repeat reminds me I need to repeat behaviors to make them a habit. I find this happens most often when the behaviors are focused on taking care of myself. I have to make sure the top activities on my daily schedule are those activities which help me rejuvenate and take care of myself. I have to make sure I don't overextend myself to take care of things others can do (of course, not as well as I could). I have to rinse and repeat to ensure I do everything possible to help me achieve a balanced and joyful life.

Rest – When it came to writing these helpful hints, I didn't write them in order. I would think about a particular letter of the day and then brainstorm a list of helpful hints starting with the letter. I would then ponder the list for a couple of days to select the three ideas I felt most comfortable writing about, so I'm not really sure how often I may have mentioned the need for rest. My guess is maybe never. I'm not a good "at rest" person. I seem to be on the go from the moment I open my eyes until the moment I crawl into bed at night. Even then, it seems I can't turn off my mind to get a good night's sleep.

As I get older, I realize how important rest is and have been trying to incorporate it into my life on a more consistent basis. I'm not just talking about physical rest but emotional and mental rest as well. I have to schedule "rest" into my calendar, but I do it. I may "rest" by doing yoga (bringing my body, mind, and spirit into a balanced state). I may "rest" by putting my feet up for 15 minutes and doing some deep breathing. I may rest by getting a massage. Each person's rest needs are different and are met in different ways. Find what it is that gives you the opportunity to rest, and then, rinse and repeat until you've made it a habit.

S

Saying goodbye – Saying goodbye always seems like a painful thing (unless it's saying goodbye to the mammography technician). Goodbye means you are discontinuing doing something and often we associate goodbye with regrets and sadness. When we're getting divorced, we're saying goodbye to our former married self and to our former spouse as a spouse. There is some grief associated with goodbye (let's not talk about the grief you endured during your marriage).

Saying goodbye is often a ritual; you may hug, make plans for future visits, and even stand in the driveway and wave as the person drives away. When some people leave, your ritual might be kicking up your heels and shouting "yahoo." But either way, right or wrong, good or bad; we need to acknowledge that saying goodbye can cause us grief and we may need a ritual to get through it.

Several months after my divorce, my daughter was with her father for the weekend, and I took the opportunity to create my ritual for saying goodbye to myself as a wife and to my former spouse. I took all the photographs, greeting cards, notes, etc. I had collected during our life together and (you thought I was going to say had a bonfire, didn't you?) I spread everything out on the floor. I looked at each item, recalled the event, and took a temperature reading about how I felt about it. This took me the entire weekend because I did not want to rush it, and I wanted to give myself permission to feel whatever it was I was feeling. Sometimes I needed tissues, sometimes I had to force myself to unclench my teeth, sometimes I laughed out loud, and sometimes I needed wine. This ritual honored me and my feelings, and it also afforded me the opportunity to say goodbye.

Seek positive guidance and help – Asking for help… why is it so difficult? I struggled with asking for help for many years. (Friends say I still do.) I think the focus here is on the word "positive." When you're feeling overwhelmed, you may be a bit reckless and desperate and reach out to any life preserver thrown your way. A good example of this is after having an extremely frustrating and overwhelming day you go to the ice cream parlor for a super double deluxe banana split. Yes, you may experience a temporary sense of enjoyment, but you are at risk for a major stomachache.

Therefore, when you're seeking guidance or help, make sure it's positive and right for you. For me to ask someone for help, it has to be someone with whom I have a relationship and someone I respect and trust.

When I sought help based on those three requirements, I actually had a very small group of people to turn to. However, I know I will always get honesty from a person who is smart, compassionate, and has good common sense, and those characteristics define the people in my go-to group.

Set an example – Yuck, just the idea of setting an example gives me the creeps; it's such a large responsibility. However, the idea of setting an example has been a gentle and nurturing concept during my divorce and the subsequent years of sharing parenting responsibilities with my former spouse. Much of the time we set an example without giving it much thought. For example, the way we open the door at the grocery store for an elder, the proper way we conduct ourselves at the dinner table, the courtesies we extend to others by lending a helping hand, and so on, and so on. These events happen with little thought on our part, but they greatly influence what our child thinks of us and how our child herself acts.

So when did I let setting an example serve as a reminder? Most often when I'm trying to resolve a conflict and when I react to what someone else does. Whether the conflict is between myself and my former spouse, my daughter's teacher, my current live-in significant other (LISO), or an overzealous salesperson, here are the steps I try to take:

1. Listen to what the other person has to say without interruption.
2. Restate what the person said in my own words to make sure we both understand what is being discussed.
3. Make a list of the mutual areas of agreement and the areas of disagreement. [Side note: You'll usually find the areas of agreement far outweigh the areas of disagreement and you're better able to focus on those few areas of disagreement successfully.]
4. Brainstorm resolutions to the areas of disagreement.
5. Agree on what might work for both of you.

6. Create a plan to implement the solution including how and when you are going to measure success.

The reason I try to take these steps is so my daughter can learn, from my example, an appropriate way to resolve conflict.

Here is a clincher – what do you do if you have to agree to disagree? It's a real possibility, especially over matters you feel strongly about. For example, let's say one parent (I won't name names here) feels it's all right for the child to sit in the front seat of a car and the other parent strongly disagrees. You proceed through step 1, 2, 3, and 4, but step 5 is a stalemate. Stop riding a dead horse, and agree to disagree. At that point, the parent who does not agree may have to make adjustments to meet his or her needs. For example, with the car situation, the parent who insists the child must ride in the back seat may have to do the bulk of transportation even if it's to and from the other parent's house. If you're unwilling to make the adjustment to provide more of the transportation, then you can't feel that strongly about the issue and should be able to achieve step 5 and 6.

"Well that's not fair," you might proclaim. Well, life isn't fair (you already know that).

And you gotta do whatcha gotta do. So set a good example, hush up, and do it. Just think; the quiet time you have in the car with your child might be more special time together.

T

There are no "should haves" – "I should have…" I never really understood this phrase because if you should have, then obviously you didn't. So I believe, "should haves" don't exist. Whatever it is you should have done, you didn't do. So ,what are we doing crying over spilled milk or milk we didn't spill but we should have? It gets confusing. If you spend time thinking about it (you know how I love to over-analyze things), you may come to the same conclusion I did. Should haves have no positive value and don't exist. So, I choose not to have them in my life.

Should haves seem to come with a negative judgment. If you should have done something and you did not, a should have suggests you regret not doing it. People, people, do you really need to add unnecessary regrets to your life right now? I have had lengthy conversations with people about should haves. (It seems I'm much more eloquent on the topic when a glass of wine is involved.) Here is my conclusion: If you should have, you didn't it, and it is over, and there is nothing you can do about it, so (say it with me), let it go.

There is always a solution – Can't never could. Won't never would. Simple statements but very powerful when you look at the perspective behind them. Can't prohibits success and invites failure. Can't closes the mind and heart and opens the door to fear. Lose the word "can't" from your vocabulary when you are looking at a concern or issue you need to resolve.

The concern can be about the divorce, yourself, your spouse, or your child. Constantly focus on the solution. Brainstorm ideas and keep massaging them until you find one that protects your child and meets your needs. It doesn't have to be perfect. It doesn't have to be forever. It just has to serve as a solution for now.

Let's talk a minute about brainstorming. Some people are under the mistaken impression that brainstorming means every idea is a good idea and you can then pick the best idea from a bucket full of good ideas. That is not true; brainstorming means any idea needs to be presented—the good, the bad, and the ugly. Often, looking at the ugly ideas helps to make the good or right idea more obvious. During a brainstorming session, there is only one rule. Evaluate the ideas not the person presenting them. When you brainstorm, write down every idea that comes to mind for the first minute or two. Then go back and look at each idea and identify the pros and cons. (Remember, you're evaluating the idea not the person.) After an analysis of the ideas, mutually decide upon the one that seems right for addressing the concern and then lay out a plan for implementing it.

There is always a solution. Commit to finding the solution. Commit to honesty and collaboration. You can do it!

Terrorism – The events of September 11, 2001 touched all of our souls with terror and sorrow, and it made me realize something about terrorism. It can be very real in our children's lives.

I've been speaking with a college friend who has been divorced for over two years. He has joint custody of his six–year old daughter, and he and his former wife are acting in a place of fear. As a result, they're unsuccessful in fulfilling their parenting responsibilities right now. I was thinking their behaviors have caused a terrorist act that will forever affect their daughter's lives. Terrorism means an act based on terror. Fear, horror, shock, and panic are all synonyms for terror. This little girl's parents are acting out of fear, and she is shocked and horrified as a result of their behaviors. They no longer communicate on a rational level. They use the child as a pawn to get "their way" with the other adult, and they manipulate and lie.

This little girl is experiencing a sense of abandonment (the parents she trusted to keep her safe have left). She is experiencing terror (there is no safe place in her world), and she is living in an environment of deceit. Her own little twin towers have been shattered; fire, hysteria, and rubble is what she struggles with every day. This is a child without a foundation, a child without hope, and there is no parent she can go to, no place she can hide, and no one who can lift her up out of the destruction and wrap her in a blanket of comfort and love. Her parents are so wrapped up in their own fear, hatred, and desire to "win," the result is their little girl loses.

I don't mean to rip your heart out of your chest or turn your stomach or even overdramatize. However, what is happening to this child is nothing short of terrorism. If you agree, keep her in mind when you are struggling to maintain love and focus in your co-parenting relationship.

U

Unusual is good – With a section of the book entitled "Weird Stories," it's probably no surprise to you that I think unusual is good. When people say to me, "That's not normal," or "You're trying to be weird," I am happy. I don't want to be normal, predictable, or typical. But that's me. How does this deal with you? It's a reminder there is more than one way to do something and its okay to look beyond normal and conventional.

As I deal with things in my life, both personally and professionally, I think about having a toolbox. I put anything I can use to help me into the toolbox so it is ready when I need it. Since people cannot know everything they will encounter in their lives, I figure I should look far and wide to get items for my toolbox.

United we stand, divided we fail – No, this is not a typo. I do not mean divided we fall. I really mean divided we fail. If you and your former spouse can unite in your commitment to provide the most loving, honest, and safe environment for your child, then you will succeed. When obstacles arise (AND THEY WILL), remember the division of your focus and commitment will result in failure for everyone involved.

Universe is listening – I want my daughter to have a spiritual connection which provides her comfort and strength. Of the many different spiritual avenues we explored, the one she most often turns to is, "the universe is listening."

The concepts associated with "the universe is listening" include the following:

1. Visualize something
2. Affirm it
3. Believe it as a reality

If you perform these steps, you have a much greater chance of fulfilling what you sought.

The first time my daughter tried it, she got a dog. She was seven years old when my adored dog passed away, and she wanted us to get another one. My heart was so broken I didn't want to get another dog. I also realized the care and training of the dog would fall into my court of responsibility, and I just didn't want to add another task to my plate. So my answer was, "No."

About eight months later, Boukie called me from work and asked if we could do a favor for a colleague of his, and without thinking, I said, "Yes." [Note to self: Reread the part in this book about gathering all of the information you need to make a good decision.] He came home from work with an adorable two–month–old Chesapeake Bay retriever puppy we were just rescuing until we could find it a good home.

When my daughter saw the puppy, she ran over, flew into my arms, and proclaimed, "The universe not only listens, Mama, it also gives you what you want." I still believe in talking to the universe, but I'm very cautious about what I ask for. You just might get it.

V

Value your network – When people go through a trauma (and let's face it, divorce is a trauma), it's not uncommon to focus on yourself. How will I juggle my schedule between work and parenting? Will anyone ever find me desirable again? Will I be able to afford doing everything I want for my child? How can I lose these extra 10 pounds? And the list goes on and on. It seems the only time we reach out to our network of friends and family is if we need something; a free babysitter, a pity–party attendee, etc.

You may want to take time and focus on the value your network provides you so you can make sure you are not taking advantage of them. After my divorce, a teenage girl down the street would come by just about every day after school to "play" with my daughter. I never asked her to stop by, but I always gave her an afterschool snack. I also offered to help her with struggling school assignments, and she did seem to really enjoy her time with my daughter. However, I never really stopped to think about her value in my network. Once I did, I discussed a more formal arrangement with her. She was thrilled to earn the little bit of money I could give her to babysit, and I could count on her to be at the house during a scheduled time so I could get some work done.

Twenty years later, I'm still in touch with my valued network neighbor and just received a Christmas card from her. It's wonderful to see her as a happy mother of three children. (With all of those kids, she probably values her network.)

Voice deal breakers – Any relationship is like a negotiation. Even the best relationships survive because of the art of compromise. When you want to make a deal with another person, you actively listen to what they are saying, try to understand their perspective, voice your position, and see if you can reach an agreement. Most times this strategy works, and you can reach a conclusion which meets everyone's needs. But every now and again, a time arises when you have a deal breaker, the one thing or set of things for which there is no compromise from your perspective.

Let's go Hollywood for a moment. Actors negotiate for various ancillary benefits when they are discussing a particular part. Let's say the actor wants a private dressing room with a gourmet chef and a personal trainer on site. The studios say okay, but in exchange, they want to hold all the financial strings for syndication. So back and forth the actor and studio negotiates. Then, all of a sudden the studio throws on the table the right they have to change the script, and it may include a nude scene. The negotiation room grows silent; the actor stands up, announces this is a deal breaker, and leaves the room.

Well, each of us has our list of deal breakers. We can justify them for whatever reason we want (safety, integrity, etc.). The list may be ludicrous from someone else's perspective, or it may be completely understandable. It doesn't matter because the bottom line is this list of items can break a deal. Each spouse needs to discuss this list with the other so you are both clear on them. This discussion is for information only. You do not have to defend your position. You don't have to negotiate. You simply have to inform so you can each avoid these deal breakers.

See, the problem with a deal breaker is it can take everything you have worked on for so long and completely destroy it. You have made wonderful strides in creating an equitable divorce. You have taken every precaution to ensure you have a kid–friendly relationship with your former spouse. You have planned every event and even have back up plans. You have invested a great deal of time, money, emotional energy, strength, courage, and commitment to create a healthy environment for all people involved. If you don't discuss your deal breakers, all of the work you've done to date could blow up in an instant and leave you in a position to start all over again, from a defeated, disheartened place.

Don't do it. Voice your deal breakers. Get all the cards out on the table. The more up front discussions and planning you do, the greater the chance you will experience "happily ever after." That's Hollywood!

Vent – Sometimes you get so angry, frustrated, or scared you think you are going to blow up. Well, go ahead, blow up. Just make sure you're in a safe place when you do it and the explosion isn't going to leave any casualties. So what does this mean? It means you find a sounding board, but hey, don't call me. I don't want the job. During the tumultuous times of a divorce, we tend to cling to our family and friends for support and encouragement. However, when your entire relationship with your family and friends centers on your divorce and every little picky thing your former spouse does, this will quickly grow more than a little old. And when you keep going on and on with this for over a year, this is not a good thing.

Of course, the first thing I would like to tell you is "let go of it, move on with your life." I know at times, it's a difficult to do. Let's focus here on what is a sounding board and where can you find one.

There is nothing as comforting as talking to a live person and getting all of their sympathies, but save those discussions for when you really, really need them. Here is what I suggest when something arises that makes you so angry, frustrated, or scared you think you are going to explode.

1. Blow up – punch a pillow, get into the shower and scream until your throat hurts, make a loaf of bread and knead it until it is in tiny little shreds. Go for it, get it out of your system. I just have to tell you my first editor on this book is a foodie and she told me

you can't knead dough into tiny shreds (just goes to show how my domestic skills shine).

2. Find an inanimate sounding board. It might be the park, the piano, a mountain top, or someplace else where you can go, talk it all out, cry if you have to, yell if you must, and yet a place where you find comfort in the surroundings. A friend of mine has playlists of music for just this occasion; she has the screeching sounds of some songs on one playlist and the soothing sounds of other songs on another (smart of her to add this to her toolbox).

3. Hold a venting ritual. Some people write down everything that is bothering them and then tear the paper into pieces and burn it (keep a fire extinguisher nearby). While others take their vents, tuck them in balloons, and set them free into the sky.

4. If you really, really must, go talk to a friend or family member, but at least keep track of the number of times you do, so you don't go overboard.

W

Want what's best – You probably think I'm going to discuss this helpful hint as it pertains to your child. No, this hint is for you. What's the best for you? What components of your life, when blended together, give you the right environment to live and love fully? Think about your physical health, your emotional health, your mental health, and your spiritual health. Think about your dreams and aspirations. Think about unresolved issues. Make a list (oh come on, you knew I was going to tell you to make a list). But this time, the list is used to help you recommit to yourself, to focus on you, to want what's best for you; so you can work towards achieving those goals.

Words are weapons – My mother used to always say, "Never say anything you wouldn't want the whole world to hear." If you think there might never be a time when the whole world is going to listen to you, think Internet where the whole world can hear. By keeping my mother's advice in the back of your mind, it will help prevent you from saying something you didn't mean, or something which can be misinterpreted, or is even hurtful. If you think about it further, when someone says something ugly, it really is more a reflection on the person who is saying it versus the person who is receiving the hateful words.

What if – What If? It's a terrible place to live, and yet we do it all the time. What if we didn't get divorced, what if we tried yet again to make the marriage work, and what if I made different choices, what if, what if, what if? You could "what if" yourself until you were crazy and still be no closer to living the fulfilling life you were meant to live. Keep your focus; lose the terms "what if" (it's just the questioning form of should have) from your vocabulary. I promise you will be happier, live more in the present, not punish yourself unnecessarily, and be freer to use your mind and heart for the matters over which you do have some control.

X

X–tra mile – You're going to have to go the extra mile; you're going to have to do some things you don't like and don't want to do. But be assured, there are many extra miles ahead of you, and those miles will have obstacles, sidetracks, and unmarked territory (not much of a pep talk, huh). Also be assured you can do this. Give yourself credit often, take time to care for yourself, keep your focus, make your plans, stay on course, and the road will bring you to where you want to go.

X*^(#*& – (I think this is what someone types when they are cussing in writing, right?) Let's say my daughter comes home after spending the weekend at her friend's house with an upset stomach. I'm the one who has to hang a pail over the side of her bed, put cool cloths on her forehead, and (please God, NO) clean up vomit in the middle of the night. I have to choose how to react to the fact that her friend's mother did not monitor her food intake, which has been confirmed by her recounting what she ate all weekend. Dear Lord, does the woman think she needs to be these kids' best friend? Does she not understand the basic food groups? Does she not know sugar is not a key food group?

I'm tired (because I'm up all night with her). I'm cranky (because this is not the first time this has happened with this woman). I'm anxious (because who wants to see their child suffering), and I'm nauseous (because, let's face it, puking is contagious). Now, are these the ideal adjectives to describe how you feel when you want to set an example for how to react to a negative situation? Well, no, but these are the ones I have, so what do you do? (You definitely want to reread the "What is Important" section.

1. Focus on what you can do. In this case, comfort your child, sing a soothing song, and help her to relax.

2. Pray for peace of mind, tolerance, and for help to remove the image of strangling your daughter's best friend's mother with your bare hands.

3. Then, tuck her in, shut off the light, and go to bed.

And if you ever wonder if you are setting an example, ask yourself "If my daughter saw me right now, would I be proud of myself?" It's a great reminder.

XOXO – Hopefully, you interpret this entire book in the spirit in which it was written; filled with hugs and kisses (well at least verbal hugs and supportive gestures). You thought this section might talk about how important it is to hug and kiss your child; but you already knew that. You might have thought I would make another plug for hugging and kissing yourself more, and I do. However, I guess this section is simply to remind you that you can do this. My heart goes out to you (along with my big mouth), but I sincerely wish you the best in your endeavors and hope this book can provide you with some loving support.

Y

You need to find you – During a major transition in your life, you may lose sight of you. I know behind all of my lists, schedules, plans, charts, and choices, there's a person who needs to feel complete and whole. There's a woman who needs to feel desirable and lovable. There's an adult who needs to feel competent and productive, and there's an inner child who needs to feel nurtured and appreciated. As you plan your day, schedule time to check in with yourself. Take a 10-minute walk around the block and ask, "How are you doing today?"

Have a phone conversation with a friend about how she might handle something you are struggling with. Go to the library and get a book about a topic you want to explore. Be sure to keep the dialog with yourself open and respectful. Finding you, developing you, and raising you to the highest level you can needs to be a priority.

You have to – This statement is coupled with "You don't have to like it." In fact, I thought the title of this book could be "You don't have to like it." The fact remains; you must maintain communications with the other parent. Communication is probably the most critical aspect of your entire relationship with him. Now listen carefully. You do not have to like this, but you have to do it. You don't like going to the dentist, but you go. You don't like paying taxes, but you pay them. You may not like having meetings with your former husband, but you will have them.

Yesterday is gone – There is just no way around it. While it is important to hold onto good memories and traditions, it is equally important to not get mired down in what was. Find a way to build new traditions and memories for the life you are creating now.

When I was growing up, Thanksgiving was a holiday that was all about tradition. This holiday included getting the entire family together, making the traditional feast, and enjoying an atmosphere of gratitude. When we moved out of state, we no longer had the proximity to all of our family members, and with only three people in the household; we didn't see the need nor had the time and expense for a traditional feast.

We decided to create a new tradition that made sense for our new life. Each year, we would pick a different country and prepare an appetizer, main course, and dessert from that country. We would make place mats using the country's flag for our design. We would also learn how to say hello, good-bye, and I love you in the native language (thank goodness for those language websites).

This new tradition gave us an opportunity explore different cultures, enjoy diverse foods, and spend time together doing something new. To this day, even if our daughter goes to her fiancée's parents' house to celebrate Thanksgiving with them, we always find time over the weekend to keep our tradition alive.

Z

Zip your lip (ZYL) – Here's a hint you'll rely on throughout your life. It is closely associated with filter your thoughts. Personally, professionally, with spouses, children, friends, family, and even associates, we have to learn to zip our lips. Someone comes to you with a problem, and being the excellent "fixer" you are, you may want to immediately tell the person exactly what he or she needs to do to take care of the problem. ZYL, at least for the moment. Step back and ask some probing questions to see if the person really wants a solution or whether he or she just wants to vent. Coupled with zipping is filtering your thoughts and zipping can really help. How many times did something come out of your mouth and your next thought was, "Did I say that out loud?" Well, ZYL helps by requiring you to explore the situation, think about things for a moment, and filter your thoughts. This allows you to carefully construct a response to address the person's need with integrity and honors their ownership of the issue.

Zap negativity – If you hear the word "choice" one more time, you'll probably scream at me. (Aren't you glad this is the end of the book?) However, negativity has no value in your life and the sooner you realize it, the happier you are going to be. I hope you realize this book had two primary objectives: the first to guide you through a constructive divorce and the second to help you heal yourself. Zapping negativity contributes to both objectives. Finding balance in every aspect of your life will give you the equilibrium to explore new things, take on new adventures, and still have peace of mind and heart.

Here is how I started zapping negativity. Whenever I would say something negative (usually about myself), I would stand up and use an imaginary eraser and erase the negativity from my head by making a circular motion three times, while saying, "Erase, erase, erase." Then, I would require myself to say three positive things about myself out loud to replace the negative thing. As you can imagine, the people in the grocery store, post office (always a good place for negative thoughts), or anywhere else where I performed this ritual thought I was nuts. Oh well. The good news is after embarrassing myself several times, I finally took the hint and was successful with zapping negativity.

Zero room for doubt – Overwhelmed? I bet you are. Anxious about how successful you will be? Who wouldn't be? Concerned you might fail at times? Of course you will fail at times. Worried you can't handle this? Sure you are. But do me a favor; heck, I spent over a year of my life writing this book, the least you can do is one little favor. Go to the mirror, look yourself in the eyes and say, "There is no room for doubt. I will endure. I will heal. I will do what's best for me and my child." If you need to repeat this little ritual every day, go for it!

WRAPPING IT UP

As I'm finishing the first draft of this book, my daughter is in the other room with her father and her fiancée, packaging a large order of chocolates that our Le Cordon Bleu chef has prepared. Yes, our daughter, at the age of 21 has graduated college, graduated from the prestigious culinary school in Paris, and has opened up her own business; quite a few accomplishments for a young woman. And yes, her father has been at our home for the past week, staying in the room across the hall from me, sharing meals, and working side by side with all of us to support our daughter. During this project, we have shared laughter, had heated discussions, experienced frustrations with temperamental labels, and even enjoyed a glass of wine together. But whatever life has thrown at us this weekend, and all of the years before, Rick and I can be proud of our efforts to create an environment that was not at our child's expense.

ACKNOWLEDGEMENTS

Every book starts with an idea that receives input along the journey to its creation. While the idea was initially mine, I could never have gotten the book to you without the resourceful contributions of Ariana Duncan and the ever-vigilant eye of my outstanding editor, MJ Plaster. But before she got her red pen on the book, other contributors included my yoga sisters, my best friend, Connie Rosano, and my terrific aunts, Lois Costantino and Sally Wynne. I am also grateful to my other editors; Shauna Ingram and Rick Gunn (yes a main character in the book). While my creative juices flowed into the words, I got stuck on the cover design so the credit and my appreciation go to Carol Martin. There are so many people who were and are important in my daughter's life and who have helped me be the best parent I could. You know who you are and I'm grateful to each of you. Which brings us up to the great team at Morgan James Publishing whose wisdom, insights, and encouragement helped in every way possible. And finally, to D, who keeps me in flowers, always makes my friends and strays feel like honored guests, and spoils me rotten; keep doing it.

ABOUT THE AUTHOR

A certified aromatherapist for more than 20 years, Judith Fitzsimmons has previously authored *Seasons of Aromatherapy* and *Aromatherapy Answers*. In her newest book, she turns her attention to another passion: constructive parenting. Judith lives in Franklin, TN, where she enjoys writing, creating aromatherapy blends, and teaching yoga.

CPSIA information can be obtained at www.ICGtesting.com
Printed in the USA
BVOW08s0009261015

424063BV00004B/110/P